TAKE SATAN TO COURT NOW!

EDDIE NAYLOR, SR.

ReadersMagnet, LLC

Take Satan to Court Now!
Copyright © 2022 by Eddie Naylor

Published in the United States of America

ISBN   Paperback: 978-1-958030-70-7
ISBN   eBook: 978-1-958030-71-4

All rights reserved. No part of this publication may be reproduced, stored in a retrieval system or transmitted in any way by any means, electronic, mechanical, photocopy, recording or otherwise without the prior permission of the author except as provided by USA copyright law.

The opinions expressed by the author are not necessarily those of ReadersMagnet, LLC.

ReadersMagnet, LLC
10620 Treena Street, Suite 230 | San Diego, California, 92131 USA
1.619. 354. 2643 | www.readersmagnet.com

Book design copyright © 2022 by ReadersMagnet, LLC. All rights reserved.

Cover design by Ericka Obando
Interior design by Dorothy Lee

Table of Contents

Introduction 7

CHAPTER ONE
Take Satan To Court, Now! 11

CHAPTER TWO
Who Is Satan? 16

CHAPTER THREE
Satan Invisible Army 18

CHAPTER FOUR
God Has Allowed Satan To Test Us 27

CHAPTER FIVE
Mankind Need A Saviour 29

CHAPTER SIX
The Three Personality Types In The Earth 32

CHAPTER SEVEN
Who Can Legally Take Satan To Court? 43

CHAPTER EIGHT
Satan Have Legal Rights Too 48

CHAPTER NINE
Satan Is A Prosecutor And Jesus Christ Is Our Defense Attorney 96

CHAPTER TEN
Blood Is Thicker Than Water 112

CHAPTER ELEVEN
It's Who You Know That Counts 120

CHAPTER TWELVE
We Know Someone Who Judges Ear 127

CHAPTER THIRTEEN
I Have A Right To Use My Savior Name.. 133
CHAPTER FOURTEEN
Our Soul Are Woven Together In Agape Love 136
CHAPTER FIFTEEN
Is Our Relationship With Jesus Real?.. 144
CHAPTER SIXTEEN
You Can Be Part Of The Family Today... 152
CHAPTER SEVENTEEN
It's A Wake-Up Call For Christians 160
CHAPTER EIGHTEEN
In Summary We Are In Spiritual Warfare Now Now!!!!!! 168

TAKE SATAN TO COURT NOW

INTRODUCTION

Satan is the great accuser of the saints. Jesus is the great defender of the saints. They are in heaven waging a relentless courtroom battle for our souls.

On one side stands Satan as *"the accuser of our brothers... who accuses them day and night before our God"* **(Revelation 12:10)**. On the other side stands Jesus as "our great high priest who has passed through the heavens" **(Hebrews 4:14),** *"who indeed is interceding for us"* **(Romans 8:34).** Both are passionately arguing their case before God the judge.

Satan is unrolling his endless scroll of charges against us. Maybe he's talking about you right now. Maybe he's talking about me. He's reminding God of our past sins. He's highlighting our present sins. He's questioning our motives. He's suggesting and speculating and slandering and accusing. He's saying smooth, believable things like, *"Does Job fear God for no reason? Have you not put a hedge around him and his house and all that he has, on every side? You have blessed the work of his hands, and his possessions have increased in the land. But stretch out your hand and touch all that he has, and he will curse you to your face"* **(Job 1:9-11).**

We cannot defend ourselves. Mainly because Satan is right — we have broken God's law excessively and we deserve severe punishment. And because even though there are some areas where Satan's accusations are false (like he falsely accused Job of having selfish motives), we aren't there to defend ourselves. Not that it would matter if we were present to give personal testimony. For every defense we might give for ourselves, our mere presence would bring 10,000 more valid accusations.

But Jesus Christ is there. He stands before His Father as the glorified God-man. He has a lifetime of perfect, confirmed, documented, human righteousness to his name. He has scars on his hands, his feet, his head, his back, and his side. As Satan rails against us and demands that God exercise justice and judgment, our defender holds out His hands before His Father. "Father, you know that it is finished. These sins have been punished. Once and for all. Let them go. They are paid for."

God the judge looks at Satan. He looks at His Son. He knows that this courtroom battle will continue until Satan is bound and finally cast into hell. But He knows what His answer will always be. He loves His Son. He loves His Son's righteousness. He loves His Son's sacrifice. And He loves His new children who have been made righteous through the death of His Son. So He hears the pleas of intercession, while Satan's shouts of accusation and demands for justice and cries of unfairness go unacknowledged once more. It's not that Satan's calls for justice carry no weight with God. It's that God has already fulfilled His justice by crushing His Own Son under its eternal weight.

Satan will try again. He will try constantly. He will question God's justice and undermine the Son's sacrifice and condemn our brothers and sisters around the world, but Jesus Christ our Mediator will speak more powerfully and persuasively. He will intercede for us by pointing to His own devastating sacrifice and pleading for God's blessing on us. And God will listen to His Son.

"Who shall bring any charge against God's elect? It is God who justifies. Who is to condemn? Christ Jesus is the one who died — more than that, who was raised — who is at the right hand of God, who indeed is interceding for us" **(Romans 8:33-34).** Why is no one able to condemn us? Because Jesus died? Yes, but more. Because Jesus was raised? Yes, but more. Because Jesus ascended to the Father and sat down at His right hand? Yes, but more. *Because of all these things, yes, but finally and decisively because Jesus is currently interceding for us.*

This is really happening in heaven. Satan is really accusing us. And Jesus is really interceding for us.

CHAPTER ONE

TAKE SATAN TO COURT, NOW!

Shortly after Lucifer, along with one-third of the angelic hosts were kicked out of heaven because of rebellion, something quite unusual took place at that very moment. Their expulsion from heaven simply means a harsh rejection from God due to their arrogance and pride. Since they were rejected by God, their holiness, perfection, as well as their goodness, could not be sustained and maintained any longer.

They all have undergone a completely strange transformation that had never occurred prior to that. They were all transformed into evil spirit. Lucifer becomes Satan, and his legions of angels become demons. In other context, Satan is just a broad term used to describe all evil being. The term Satan means adversary; in other words, the one who is always there to oppose God and His people.

Notably, there is no restoration for him. That's what draws a clear distinction between the fall of Lucifer and his legions of angels and the fall of humankind. The bottom line is that God has done something that truly transcended the history of humanity on behalf of all of us that He hasn't done for the fallen angels. God had already had a plan to bring humanity back to Him through Christ before they even fell into sin. That plan was a mystery for Satan.

This simply means that as long we're alive, we're in an infinitely better position than Satan because we still have the opportunity to be saved and inherit eternal life through Jesus alone. Since the devil has a hold on every individual who is not saved yet, so they are left with the responsibility to choose whom they are willing to serve.

16For this is the way God loved the world: He gave His one and only Son, so that everyone who believes in Him will not perish but have eternal life. (**John 3:16**)

If we're willing to take our responsibility on the basis of acknowledging that we're wretched sinners in the sight of a holy and righteous God and run to Christ, we will surely be restored. God will intervene in our lives, justify us, cleanse us, sanctify us, and then transform us into the person whom He wants us to be.

On top of that, He will equip us for the purpose of not only living a holy life but to carry out His work on this earth. Unfortunately, Satan is in a completely desperate situation because he has already been judged and condemned by God. Consequently, his final destination and his demons is the Lake of fire (**Matthew 25:41; Revelation 20:14**).

So, The Question is Why Does Satan Hate Humanity up to Core? Why is he Making Sure That Nobody Gets Saved?

First of all, when thinking about Satan's attitude toward mankind, one thing that we might say to ourselves is that humanity didn't cause Satan to lose his position in heaven. Therefore, why going after humanity in such a wrathful manner? The main reason is that Satan has found himself in a highly desperate situation, and he is trapped between both his past and his future. He cannot go back and take full responsibility for his rebellion in order for him to be restored by God. At the same time, there is a horrible judgment pronounced against him that will eventually take place at some point during his existence that he cannot escape. He is well aware of the fact that there is no restoration for him, and his time is running short day-by-day (**Revelation 12:12**).

Since he can't go back to heaven in order to take revenge against God Almighty who kicked him out of heaven; Satan in his arrogance, pride, and full hatred toward God wants to unleash his evil sentiments toward someone. As a result, he has embraced an approach to bring destruction to anything deemed valuable to God. Bear in mind, Satan's initial plan was to supersede God, and his desire to do so far excelled his very being as just a created being. We can conclude that Satan harbors a hatred toward God, along with humanity that far excels his own nature. That hatred is the key factor that motivates him daily in his quest to further corrupt and destroy humanity. He's totally obsessed with doing so; his main weapon is sin.

The Bible tells us in (**Genesis 1:26**) that God has made us in His image, which demonstrates that we're very important and special to God. However, it's not something that can be taken for granted either because our significance only relies on our Maker. Because if we're detached from God who is the source of our life because of sins, that significance we possess doesn't matter that much.

To answer that question, there are several reasons as to why that Satan hates us so much. The first reason is that we're made in the image of God Almighty. The second one is that God has granted us an unmerited privilege that the enemy doesn't have. We have such a mind-blowing opportunity to go to heaven and be with our Maker forever through Christ by escaping his control. That's truly what has intensified even further that hatred.

The truth is that he had been there, and he knows what heaven is truly like. He knows the extraordinary beauty that dwells in that place, and so forth. Consequently, his main goal is to ensure that nobody ever goes to that place. He wouldn't want anybody to inherit what he has lost. Here is the deal, if you can't make it to heaven, then you will have to accompany him to where he's destined to spend his eternity.

HOW DOES HE CARRY OUT HIS SCHEMES?

He does that by hardening men's heart so that they don't accept the message of the gospel. It all starts by keeping people in their lost condition indefinitely for the purpose of not only destroying their souls but to use them in order to fulfill his agenda.

He blinds people's eyes and minds so that they cannot see the light of the gospel that displays the glory of Christ, who is the image of God (**2 Corinthians 4:4**). He blinds people's minds toward the truth trough immoral living and false beliefs. He Influences people to rebel against God. Moreover, he influences people to believe that they should have freedom for the sole purpose of doing whatever they want.

He manipulates people into believing that they can live their lives however they like without giving them much time to think about <u>the consequences of their sinful lifestyles</u>. He imprints that deceptive belief in people's mind that the Word of God is all about keeping them from having fun. The Word of God is all about men trying to control other people's lives. He holds them captive into sinful living. And he influences people to become very negligent and ignorant about their own eternity in the sense of being unwilling to accept Christ as their personal Savior.

He influences people to believe that they still have plenty of time ahead of them to accept Christ. He influences them to believe that they can't afford to accept Christ because the moment they do so, they will have no choice but to abandon the very things that they used to enjoy greatly. <u>His main field is deception</u>; consequently, he uses that mainly to influence people to believe in something untrue.

His plan is to bring about as much destruction, and suffering as he can to humanity. He makes people's life so miserable up to the point they even start wondering whether there is a God that loves and cares about them. He influences people to destroy their own lives as well as their souls through sinful living. Lastly, he also influences people to destroy other people's lives through violence, jealousy, envy, hatred, war, and so forth.

After all, Satan is a very wicked, vile, and destructive being. It does not bother him at all to bring utter destruction to every aspect of people's life. In other words, people's lives have no importance at all to him. It's important to also realize that, **S**atan is an opportunist. He knows that he is unable to bring about his destructive agenda to humanity all by himself; thereby, he exploits people's weaknesses.

As mentioned above, Satan's main agenda is to drag humanity to eternal destruction along with himself. Shockingly, he makes use of people in order to accomplish that. In many cases, he inspires influential people in order to bring forth all kind of bad doctrines, ideologies, philosophies, beliefs, and so forth in a way to deceive as many people as he can. Surprisingly, many people who are ensnared in his trap don't even realize that he really exists. Or they don't even realize that they are being used by him.

WHAT SHOULD BE OUR OWN RESPONSIBILITY WITH RESPECT TO DEALING WITH HIM?

Nobody has the power to fight against Satan. By the way, you cannot fight an enemy that you cannot even see. At the same time, you can't also allow yourself to continue to follow his deceptive path that will certainly lead you to destruction. Just as God has a plan for humanity, so is the devil. He cannot stop thinking about harming mankind. Our responsibility is to turn our back completely on him by coming to God.

We're commanded as believers to be mindful of his schemes (**1 Peter 5:8-9**). We're also told by the Word of God to resist him (**James 4:7**). If you're an unbeliever this does not apply to you because you cannot win that war apart from God. Your only hope is to come out of his kingdom of darkness, which is the very embodiment of eternal death by transitioning into God's glorious kingdom through Christ.

YOU MUST TAKE SATAN TO COURT TO GET FREE!!!

CHAPTER TWO

WHO IS SATAN?

People's beliefs concerning Satan range from the silly to the abstract—from a little red guy with horns who sits on your shoulder urging you to sin, to an expression used to describe the personification of evil. The Bible, however, gives us a clear portrait of who Satan is and how he affects our lives. Put simply, the Bible defines Satan as an angelic being who fell from his position in heaven due to sin and is now completely opposed to God, doing all in his power to thwart God's purposes.

Satan was created as a holy angel. Isaiah 14:12 possibly gives Satan's pre-fall name as Lucifer. Ezekiel 28:12-14 describes Satan as having been created a cherub, apparently the highest created angel. He became arrogant in his beauty and status and decided he wanted to sit on a throne above that of God (Isaiah 14:13-14; Ezekiel 28:15; 1 Timothy 3:6). Satan's pride led to his fall. Notice the many "I will" statements in Isaiah 14:12-15. Because of his sin,

God permanently removed Satan from his exalted position and role.

Satan became the ruler of this world and the prince of the power of the air (John 12:31; 2 Corinthians 4:4; Ephesians 2:2). He is an accuser (Revelation 12:10), a tempter (Matthew 4:3; 1 Thessalonians 3:5), and a deceiver (Genesis 3; 2 Corinthians 4:4; Revelation 20:3). His very name means "adversary" or "one who opposes." Another of his titles, the devil, means "slanderer."

Even though he was cast out of heaven, he still seeks to elevate his throne above God. He counterfeits all that God does, hoping to gain the worship of the world and encourage opposition to God's kingdom. Satan is the ultimate source behind every false cult and world religion. Satan will do anything and everything in his power to oppose God and those who follow God. However, Satan's destiny is sealed—an eternity in the lake of fire (Revelation 20:10).

CHAPTER THREE

SATAN INVISIBLE ARMY

Genesis 6:1-3 tells of the time before the Great Flood when certain angels rebelled against God, exchanged their angelic form for human form and began having children with human women. **Genesis 6:4** calls these children the NEPHILIM. They had human bodies. They apparently had incredible skills and abilities and eventually led the whole world astray. Before long the entire creation had been irreparably corrupted. Because they were half angels and half human the human part was destroyed in the flood and the angels part became demons.

Then the Lord said, "My Spirit will not contend with humans forever, for they are mortal; their days will be a hundred and twenty years" **(Genesis 6:3)**

NOAH AND HIS FAMILY NOT CORRUPTED

Noah and his family had not been genetically corrupted by this hybrid invasion. The Lord commissioned him and his sons to build an ark to preserve themselves, their wives, and selected animals and 120 years after His Pronouncement He destroyed the whole world in the Great Flood.

The Hebrew word translated "contend" in Genesis 6:3 means "to act as a judge". In other words the role of the Holy Spirit in pre-flood times was to convict the world of guilt in regard to sin, and righteousness, and judgment just like He's doing in our time (John 16:8). And before the flood God said there would come a time when His Spirit would step aside and allow a time of judgment to proceed, just like Paul said the restrainer would do at the end of the age.

When Satan fell, one-third of the angelic host joined him in his rebellion. These angels who fell with Satan are now known as demons. Hell was prepared for Satan and his angels. Demons and fallen angels are used interchangeably in the Bible.

The subject of demons is very real according to the Bible. The word demon is not found in Scripture, but it means evil spirit or devil. The word devil is used of Satan, the prince of demons **(Matt. 9:34; 2:24).** He is the chief evil spirit and the original source of evil in the universe. The Greek word for devil used in connection with Satan is <u>DIABOLOS</u>, meaning adversary, false accuser, slanderer, devil. It is translated "false accuser" and "slanderer" and is used of men in **1 Tim. 3:11; 2 Tim. 3:3; Titus 2:3**. It is translated devil once when applied to Judas when he became an adversary of Christ **(John 6:70)**. In thirty-four other places it is used of Satan as the chief adversary of God and is translated devil.

In the other seventy-six places where the words devil and devils are found, they refer to evil spirits or demons and the word is derived from two different Greek words, <u>DIAMONION AND DIAMON</u>, meaning evil spirits of devils. <u>THERE IS ONLY ONE DEVIL BUT THERE ARE MANY DEMONS</u>.

THE DEVIL HAS AN ANGELIC BODY AND CANNOT ENTER BODILY INTO ANYONE BUT DEMONS ARE DISEMDODIED (having no body) SPIRIT <u>and do not seem to</u>

<u>be able to operate in the material world except through possession of men and beasts who have bodies for them to operate through.</u>

THE NATURE OF DEMONS

The purpose of demons is to possess individuals

In studying the nature of demons we found that:

They are evil **(Judges 9:2); (1 Sam. 18:9-10)**; intelligent and wise **(1 Tim. 4:1; 1 Kings 22:22-24; Acts 16:16)**; powerful **(Mark 5:1-18)**; disembodied spirits **(Rev. 16:13-16)**; not angels **(Acts 23:8-9)**; not human, for they possess men and can be cast out **(Matt. 10:7; Mark 16:17)**; and are individuals **(Mark 16:9)** they have knowledge **(Matt. 9:29; Luke 4:41; Acts 19:15)**; They have faith **(Jas. 2:19)**; they have feelings **(Matt. 8:29; Mark 5:7)**; they have fellowship **(1 Cor. 10:20-21)**; they have doctrines **(1 Tim. 4:1)**; they have wills **(Matt. 12:43-45)**; they have miraculous powers **(Rev. 16:13-16)**; they have intelligence **(1 Tim. 4:1; 1 John 4:1-6)**; they have emotions **(Acts 8:7)**; they have desires **(Matt. 8:28-31)**; and other soul and spirit faculties.

THE WORK OF DEMONS

The work of demons is many. They possess people and cause:

Dumbness and deafness **(Matt. 9:32-33; Mark 9:25)**; they cause blindness **(Matt. 12:22)**; they cause grievous vexation **(Matt. 15:22)**; they cause lunacy and mania **(Matt. 4:23-24; 17:14-21;Mark 5:1-18)**; they cause uncleanness *(called unclean spirits twenty-one times,* **Luke 4:36)**; they cause someone to have supernatural strength **(Mark 5:1-18)**; they cause someone to commit suicide **(Matt. 17:15; John 10:10)**; they cause someone to have fits **(Mark 9-20)**;they cause someone to have lusts **(John 8:44; Eph. 2:1-3; 1 John 2:15-17)**; the cause counterfeit worship **(Lev. 17:7; Deut. 32:17; 2 Chron. 11:15; Ps. 106:37; 1 Cor. 10:30; Rev. 9:20)**; they cause error **(1 John 4:1-6; 1 Tim. 4:1)**; they cause sicknesses and diseases **(Matt. 4:23-24; Acts 10:38)**; they cause torments **(Matt. 4:23-24; Matt. 15:22)**; they cause deceptions **(1 Tim. 4:1-2; 1 John 4:1-6)**; they cause lying **(1 Kings 22:21-24)**;

they cause enchantments and witchcraft **(2 Chron. 33:6)**; they cause heresies **(1 Tim. 4:1)**; the cause false doctrines **(1 Tim. 4:1)**; they cause wickedness **(Luke 11:26)**; they cause fear **(2 Tim. 1:7)**; they cause worldliness **(1 John 2:15-17; 1 Cor. 2:12)**; they cause bondage **(Rom. 8:15)**; they cause discord **(Matt. 13:39; 1 Kings 22:21-24)**; they cause violence **(Matt. 17:15)**; they cause betrayals **(John 13:2; 1 Kings 22:22-23)**; they cause oppression **(Acts 10:38)**; they cause sin **(John 8:44; 1 John 3:8)**; they cause persecution **(Rev. 2:10; 1 Pet. 5:8)**; they cause jealousy **(1 Sam. 16:14; 18:8-10)**; they cause false prophecy **(1 Sam. 18:8-10; 1 Kings 22:21-24)**; and causes every evil they possibly can to come to man and God.

DEMONS CAN:

Teach **(1 Tim. 4:1)**; steal **(Matt. 13:19; Luke 8:12)**; fight **(Eph. 4:27; 6:10-18; 1 Pet. 5:8)**; get mad **(Matt. 8:28; Rev. 12:12)**; tell fortunes **(Lev. 20:27; Acts 16:16)**; be friendly (called familiar spirits sixteen times, **Lev. 20:6,27**); <u>can go out and come back into men as they will, unless cast out and rejected</u> **(Matt. 12:43-45)**; travel **(1 Kings 22:21-24; Mark 5:7,12)**; speak **(Mark 1:34; 5:12; Acts 8:7)**; imitate departed dead **(2 Sam. 28:3-9; 1 Chron. 10:13; Isa. 8:19; Deut. 18:11)**; and do many things when in possession of bodies through whom they operate.

THEY ARE CALLED:

Devils **(Mark 16:17)**; familiar spirits **(Lev.20:6)**; unclean spirits **(Mark 1:27)**; evil spirits **(Luke 7:21)**; seducing spirits **(1 Tim 4:1)**; and other things.

<u>THEY ARE MADE SUBJECT TO CHRIST AND BELIEVERS BY THE ATONEMENT, THE NAME OF JESUS, AND THE HOLY SPIRIT</u> **(Matt. 8:16-17; 12:28; Mark 16:17; Luke 10:17); Acts 19:15)**.

<u>THOUSANDS OF THEM CAN ENTER INTO AND TAKE POSSESSION OF ONE MAN AT THE SAME TIME</u> **(Mark 5:9)**.

<u>THEY MUST BE DISCERNED, TESTED, RESISTED, AND REJECTED BY BELIEVERS</u> **(1 John 4:1-6; 1 Cor. 12:10; Eph. 5:27; 6:10-18; 1 Pet. 5:8-9).**

<u>THEY ARE POSSESSED OF MORE THAN ORDINARY INTELLIGENCE</u> **(Matt. 8:29);**

<u>THEIR RIGHTFUL PLACE IS IN THE ABYSS</u> (Luke 8:31; Rev. 9:1-21);

<u>THEY HAVE A PERSONALITY</u> **(Luke 8:26-33);** are disembodied **(Matt. 12:43-45);** are Satan's <u>EMISSARIES</u> **(Matt. 12:26-?);** and are numerous **(Mark 5:9).** They enter into and control both men and beasts **(Mark 5:1-18)** and seek embodiment **(Matt. 12:43-45; Luke 8:32).** Demons possession and demon influence are different **(Matt. 4:23-24 with 16:21-23).** They know their fate **(Matt.8:31-32)** and those who have power over them **(Acts 19:29-47);** They fear God **(Jas. 2:19);** Inflict physical maladies **(Matt. 12:22; 17:15-?);** war on saints **(Eph. 6:10-18)** and influences men **(1 Tim. 4:1-5; 2 Pet. 2:10-12).** All unbelievers are more or less possessed with them **(Eph. 2:1-3).**

THE ONLY RESOURCES AGAINST DEMONS

The only resources against them are prayer, bodily control, and the whole armour of God **(Matt. 17:21, Eph. 6:10-18).**

THERE ARE DEMON SPIRITS FOR EVERYTHING

There are demon spirits for every sickness, unholy trait, and doctrinal error known among men.

<u>THEY MUST BE CAST OUT IN ORDER TO GET RELIEF FROM THEM</u>. Disease germs, which come into the bodies of men bringing them to death. Just as refuse breeds maggots, so man in his fallen state of corruption breeds germs through Unclean living and through contact with corruption in the fallen world. They are agents of Satan, corruption in the bodies of his victims.

TRAFFIC WITH DEMON SPIRITS IS FORBIDDEN IN BOTH TESTAMENTS

Traffic with demon spirits is forbidden in both Testaments **(Lev. 19-31; 20:6; Deut. 18:10; Isa. 8:19-21; 1 Chron. 10:13-14; Luke 4:41; Acts 16:16; 1 Tim. 1-5; 2 Pet. 2:1-3; 1 John 4:1-6).**

HOW DOES DEMONS ENTER INTO MEN OTHER THAN BIRTH?

There are many ways that demons can enter a human being other than those that come as a <u>PACKAGE DEAL TO EVERY HUMAN BEING</u>. Demons can enter through and be invited in:

(1) By different media

(2) By sexual perversion

(3) By immorality

(4) By New Age occult

(5) By witchcraft, astrology, seance

(6) By playing games such as dungeon and dragon, Ouija board

(7) By hypnosis

(8) By music

(9) By dancing

(10) By keeping bad company (passed from person to person)

(11) By contagious diseases

(12) By disobedience to the Word of God

(13) By negative emotions

(14) By unconsciousness

(15) By childhood experiences

(16) By heredity

(17) By bad habits

(18) By ignorance and not knowing the truth

(19) By traditions

(20) By psychology

(21) By rituals

(22) By teaching and education

(23) and by many other subtle ways

DEALING WITH THE SIN NATURE IN MAN

We will never completely solve any of our individual, family, society, national or international problem without dealing with the sin nature in man. And the only way that we can deal successfully with the sin problem is through Jesus Christ.

Revelation 16:13-16

¹³ And I saw three unclean spirits like frogs [come] out of the mouth of the dragon, and out of the mouth of the beast, and out of the mouth of the false prophet.

¹⁴ For they are the spirits of devils, working miracles, [which] go forth unto the kings of the earth and of the whole world, together them to the battle of that great day of God Almighty.

¹⁵ Behold, I come as a thief. Blessed [is] he that watcheth, and keepeth his garments, lest he walk naked, and they see his shame.

¹⁶ And he gathered them together into a place called in the Hebrew tongue Armageddon.

NOT ANGELS

For they are disembodied spirits.

Acts 23:8

⁸ For the Sadducees say that there is no resurrection, neither angel, nor spirit: but the Pharisees confess both.

⁹ And there arose a great cry: and the scribes [that were] of the Pharisees part arose, and strove, saying, We find no evil in this man: but if a spirit or an angel hath spoken to him, let us not fight against God.

Psalms 107:20

[20] He sent his word, and healed them, and delivered [them] from their destructions.

DEMONS WORK BEHIND THE SCENES

Although demons delight in causing human suffering and make it their particular goal to do just that, normally they do so behind the scenes. It is unusual for one's home to be infested with physical manifestations of the demonic.

THE PRIMARY BATTLE IS FOR THE MIND

<u>The primary battle is for the mind. If demons can gain control of a person's mind, they cannot only cause temporal suffering (which as I mentioned before they delight in immensely), but they can also cause their ultimate particular goal. Namely, through the mind, they gain the soul.</u> In this realm of spiritual warfare, we find poor souls who are addicted to sex, drugs and pornography. Here we find hearts filled with hatred, unforgiveness and thoughts of malice towards their fellow man. We find rapists, murderers, adulterers and fornicators. The list goes on.

Here lies the true battle. It is far less dangerous, although much more frightening, to deal with external manifestations of the demonic. The true danger lies in the day-to-day interactions with demons of which we are often not even aware.

MY SINCERE HOPE IS THAT MANKIND WAKE UP TO THE REALITY OF THIS UNSEEN BATTLE

My sincere hope is that mankind wake up to the reality of this unseen battle, "for our struggle is not against flesh and blood, but against the rulers, against the powers, against the world forces of this darkness, against the spiritual forces of wickedness in the heavenly places." **(Ephesians 6:12).** In other words, we are not fighting flesh and blood. Either we are fighting demons with the power of God or we are being defeated by them. Either way, the battle is real. Either way, the stakes are eternal.

THEIR ULTIMATE GOAL: THE DAMNATION OF SOULS

Brothers and sisters, make no mistake about it: Although demons delight in causing temporal suffering, there is no greater satanic rejoicing in addressed it thus far, sometimes it is dangerous to wrestle with trying to figure out why demons do what they do. The actions of demons are often without meaning and have no purpose. For instance, in the case of a violent haunting, one who finds their bed consistently shaking at night may ask the question, "is this to keep me from sleep?" or, "Did I commit some sin in this bed that gives the demon a right to do this?" These types of questions are useless, for even if we know the answers (stressing again that often there are no answers) the methods for dealing with the problem remain the same. Therefore, the real issue here is not "what is the reason". Rather, it is "What are we going to do about it?"

I can in all truthfulness that I myself have given into the temptation to try to figure out the motives for the actions of the demonic. I can therefore say with some authority that it is at best unproductive. At worst, you will drive yourself crazy trying to figure out a puzzle that cannot be solved. Rather than simply saying, "For no reason at all", I think that we can safely say that it is simply their nature to cause suffering in any possible way. If shaking someone's bed causes fear (a form of suffering and torment), then this will be an action that demons will perform because it is their nature to do so.

WE MUST TAKE SATAN TO COURT.

THEIR ULTIMATE GOAL OF SATAN AND DEMONS IS: THE DAMNATION OF SOULS.

THE ULTIMATE GOAL GOD IS SALVATION THROUGH CHRIST JESUS.

CHAPTER FOUR

GOD HAS ALLOWED SATAN TO TEST US

God has allowed Satan to test men in order to purify and refine them and to teach certain lessons in their training for the future life, but God has always delivered these men when the test was ended. God has always been the deliverer of His people in any trouble, regardless of the cause of the trouble. God is not the kind of person deliberately to bring upon His people afflictions just to have a chance to deliver them. God, however, takes pleasure in delivering His people from the hand of the enemy when the call upon Him.

These are the general purpose which God has in allowing Satan to continue:

The lease on the Earth that was giving to Adam and which Satan took form Adam has not yet run out.

To develop character and faith in the believer **(Jas. 1:12; 1 Pet. 1:7-13; 2 Pet. 1:4-9; Jude 20:24).**

To keep him humble **(2 Cor. 12:7).**

To provide conflict that saints may be rewarded through overcoming **(1 John 2:13; 4:1-6; Rev. 2:7, 11, 17, 26-28; 3:5, 12, 21).**

To demonstrate the power of God over the power of Satan **(Eph. 2:7; 3:10; 2 Cor. 4:9; Mark 16:17-20).**

To use him in afflicting people to bring them to repentance **(1 Cor. 5:1-6; 2 Cor. 2:5-11; Job 33:14-30).**

To purge man of all possibility of falling in the eternal future **(Rev. 21).**

CHAPTER FIVE
MANKIND NEED A SAVIOUR

Mankind was created sinless and perfect and given dominion over all the works of God's hands. He was supposed to rule for God and to continue in righteousness and true holiness. He was supposed to protect his dominion from outlaws and all intruders who were enemies of God and man. He was fully enlightened as to the will of the Creator. The law as well as the penalty for breaking the law was made clear. Man was trusted to obey God and do His will.

Man sinned and forfeited his right to life and fellowship with God. By his own consent he submitted his dominion to the devil and evil spirit forces who took advantage of man and his morally fallen nature and weakness to resist. The penalty for sin was death. The penalty had to be paid, and God's moral law and His adherence to moral law had to be upheld. Man could not pay the penalty and still go free, for he had not the power to take his life up again should he die and pay the penalty. If he paid the penalty he must remain forever dead. If man was to become reconciled to God and go free, some substitute had to be found to take man's place and fully meet the demands of the law. This substitute had to be more than man in order to take man's place. He had to be more than a man to be able to rise from the dead after paying the penalty, else he would remain forever dead. He must be someone who would willingly take man's place, for it would have been unjust of God to force anyone to die against his will. He had to be a sinless person, for if he were a sinner he would have to die for his own sin only. He could not have also died for all other sinners. He also had to be a federal representative of all men like Adam; else he could not have propitiated God for all men.

Fallen man could not have provided such a being. He must come from God. God could not create a being for the express purpose of having Him die for a sinner, else He would have been charged with injustice by all other free moral agents, especially His enemies. If God was to have men on the Earth to carry out His original purpose. He must either let the sinner pay his own penalty and remain forever dead and He must create another man to take the place of the original man, or He must Himself take the place of the original man, so that he could go free. This latter plan was the one God chose, for if He had chosen the first plan, the second man might have sinned as did the first. In that event, God's plan would have been no further along. Of course, this latter plan was the original plan of God, for He made man on a low plane and placed him on probation and planned that if he fell, a Savior would be provided so that all who would accept His substitutionary work for them could go free.

In this way God would be free from any charge of injustice, and His Own Being and form of government would be magnified before all free moral agents in all eternity. In this way man could be retried, tested, and given another probationary chance to prove true so that finally God's purpose concerning man and the Earth could be realized. Now no free moral agent can accuse God of being a tyrant or unjust to any person, for God did not create an innocent victim to take a sinner's place, nor demand that somebody else do something He would not do Himself. Neither did He take the rebel's life nor judge him without giving him a chance to make good and become reconciled if he so desired. God Himself took man's place and took the full penalty and met the demands of justice, thereby demonstrating His love and mercy. By this act of taking the rebel's place, God silenced forever all mouths in any form of accusation against Him and His dealings with His own creation; and by this act He fully upheld the demands of law and justice and proved that He is merciful and loving to all offenders and would give them another chance to prove themselves worthy of His great love.

For the sake of upholding the law and maintaining His government over all free wills in the universe, God could not have lessened the penalty or have been lenient with sin in any form. Otherwise, there would have been no end to a demand on such leniency by free wills who wished to sin. The law had to be upheld. Yet it certainly was not unjust for God to uphold the law and still have mercy by paying the penalty Himself, therefore giving the rebels a chance of permanent reconciliation.

THAT IS WHY ALL BORN-AGAIN BELIEVERS IN JESUS CHRIST CAN TAKE SATAN TO COURT!

CHAPTER SIX

THE THREE PERSONALITY TYPES IN THE EARTH

JESUS CHRIST DIVIDED MANKIND INTO THREE PERSONALITY TYPES AND YOU ARE ONE OF THESE TYPES, AFTER READING ABOUT THEM CAN YOU LOCATE WHICH TYPE YOU ARE?

ROMANS 12:1-2

¹I appeal to you therefore, brothers, by the mercies of God, to present your bodies as a living sacrifice, holy and acceptable to God, which is your spiritual worship. ²Do not be conformed to this world, but be transformed by the renewal of your mind, that by testing you may discern what is the will of God, what is good and acceptable and perfect.

NATURAL MAN

1 Corinthians 2:14

King James Version

¹⁴ But the natural man receiveth not the things of the Spirit of God: for they are foolishness unto him: neither can he know them, because they are spiritually discerned.

1. THE NATURAL MAN: He is born into the human family and lives in his natural state without being a child of God **(John 3:1-8; Galatians 3:26; 1 John 2:22-23; 1 John 3:9-10; 1 John 4:3; 1 John 1:7)**. He does not have the Holy Spirit of God in Him and lives his life driven by three human motivators: the lust of the flesh, lust of the eyes, and pride **(1 John 2:15-17)**. He is unable to know, much less understand the deep things of God, because He does not have the Spirit of God in Him that gives Him Spiritual wisdom. Therefore, He considers Spiritually Godly things to be foolishness and rejects God and His Word, which results in His destruction and rejection by God from having eternal life with God **(Romans 1:18-32; 1 Corinthians 2:11, 14; James 1:23-24; 1 Thessalonians 2:13-16; 1 Peter 2:9-17; Revelation 14:9-10)**.

SPIRITUAL MAN

1 Corinthians 2:15-16

King James Version

¹⁵ But he that is spiritual judgeth all things, yet he himself is judged of no man.

¹⁶ For who hath known the mind of the Lord, that he may instruct him? but we have the mind of Christ.

2. THE SPIRITUAL MAN: He is one that is born again into God's family and lives in a Spiritual state. Unlike the natural man, he does have the Holy Spirit in him, Whom he received at the moment of salvation when he trusted Christ as his Savior. He is born again as a child of God by his faith in Christ **(Galatians 3:26)**. He is able to know the deep things of God because the Holy Spirit has revealed them to Him **(Isaiah 11:2; Daniel 2:19-23; 1 Corinthians 2:4, 9-11; Ephesians 1:15-22)**. Because he has the

Spirit of God in him, he has a new nature that is not driven by the lust of the flesh, lust of the eyes, and pride **(Romans 5:5-9; 2 Corinthians 5:16-19; Galatians 6:15)**. Because He is born again by trusting Christ as His Savior, He will be saved from God's wrath to spend an eternity with God **(Psalms 2:2; Romans 1:18; Romans 5:9; Ephesians 5:6; 1 Thessalonians 1:10; 1 Thessalonians 2:13-16)**.

CARNAL MAN

1 Corinthians 3:1-3

King James Version

³ And I, brethren, could not speak unto you as unto spiritual, but as unto carnal, even as unto babes in Christ.

² I have fed you with milk, and not with meat: for hitherto ye were not able to bear it, neither yet now are ye able.

³ For ye are yet carnal: for whereas there is among you envying, and strife, and divisions, are ye not carnal, and walk as men?

3. THE CARNAL MAN: He is one that is born again into God's family, but lives and behaves as a man in a natural state living according to his carnal or fleshly desires. Instead of following the leading of the Holy Spirit, he chooses to allow the lust of the eyes, lust of the flesh, and pride tempt him, which produces ungodly works and the inability to grow in Spiritual maturity and discernment **(Romans 7:14-25; 1 Corinthians 3:1-14)**. Only by immersing himself in the Word of God and putting off the works of the flesh can he abstain from his fleshly lusts and live a life that is pleasing to God and serves as a glorification of God before unbelievers **(1 Peter 2:11-12)**. <u>Sadly, the carnal man often claims he is a Christian, but demonstrates to the world that Christians are no different than anyone else.</u>

SATAN ATTACKS PAUL

PAUL IS A CHRISTIAN AND IS DOING WHAT HE DOES NOT WANT TO DO IN HIS MIND

The truth about Romans 7 – doing what I do not want to do

Romans 7:14-25 does not describe a non-believer, or a believer that is living according to the flesh. It describes a victorious disciple.

It says in Romans 7:15, *"15For what I am doing, I do not understand. For what I will to do, that I do not practice; but what I hate, that I do."*

What Paul is saying here can seem a bit strange – why would you do what you do not understand? But Paul is not speaking about willfully committing sin (consciously giving in to the desires of the flesh.

Sin is anything that goes against God's will and His laws. To commit sin is to transgress or disobey these laws. The lust to sin dwells in human nature. In other words, it is contaminated and motivated by the sinful…). Because when you willfully commit sin, you know and understand quite well what you are doing.

Romans 7:23 – "Another law in my members"

Paul was living a crucified life. He was not serving the law of sin with his mind. (Romans 7:25.) To the extent that he had light*, he delighted in the law of God in the inward man. (Romans 7:22.)

That meant that he delighted in love, in goodness, in mercy – that was his attitude of mind. In those areas where he had received light, he crucified sin in his body. His mind that was serving God stopped these sinful desires.

THERE WERE MANY AREAS IN PAUL'S LIFE WHERE HE HAD NOT YET RECEIVED LIGHT

However, there were many areas in Paul's life where he had not yet received light. Here he was taken captive by the law of sin in his flesh, so that he did things that he hated. *"23But I see another law in my members, warring against the law of my mind, and bringing me into captivity to the law of sin which is in my members."* Romans 7:23.

Someone who is willfully committing sin is not doing what he hates, because his mind approves of it. When desire has conceived, it gives birth to sin. Conception takes place when we consent to the desire with our mind – then sin is born. (James 1:14-15.) Such a person is serving the law of sin with his *mind*.

PAUL WAS NOT WRITING ABOUT THIS KIND OF SIN

Paul was not writing about this kind of sin in Romans 7. He was serving the law of *God* with his *mind*, but at the same time, sin that was still present in his *flesh* would manifest itself without his approval – he was serving the law of *sin* with his *flesh*. These reactions from the flesh could come as THOUGHTS OR FEELINGS that he had to battle down (temptation), or as actual actions or words, which never passed his consciousness as a temptation. He received light about these later, realizing they weren't according to God's will, and therefore something he hated ("deeds of the body").

The law is spiritual, but Paul found that he was carnal, sold under sin. With his mind he served God, but he also noticed that nothing good dwelt in his flesh. (Romans 7:18.) So, *with his flesh* he couldn't do anything other than to serve the law of sin. His mind (which served God) was against his flesh (which served sin), and this created an opposition of will in his body. (Romans 7:23.)

IT WASN'T PAUL (HIS CONSCIOUS MIND) WHO DID THE THINGS HE HATED

"17But now it is no longer I who do it but sin that dwells in me." Romans 7:17. It wasn't Paul (his conscious mind) who did the things he hated, but it was sin that dwelled in him (his flesh). He hadn't seen it; he hadn't received light over it. That is why he exclaims, *"Oh wretched man that I am! Who will deliver me from this body of death?"* Romans 7:24.

The mindset of a disciple

Paul answers his own question: *"I thank God – through Jesus Christ our Lord!"* Romans 7:25. Before Jesus overcame and left us with an example to follow, it was not possible for mankind to completely overcome all sin in the flesh. But Jesus has now given us the Holy Spirit, who can show us the way through the flesh.

Like Paul, when we have repented and begun to serve God, we have a new mindset, and it is no longer we who serve sin. What comes from our flesh is not done willfully.

When we are in Christ Jesus and serve the law of God with our mind, there is no condemnation if we do the things we hate. (Romans 8:1.) We aren't condemned for being tempted (thinking thoughts or having feelings enticing us to sin), nor for actions we may have done which haven't passed our conscious mind first, so we could make a choice.

Even so, it is written that we need to put to death or mortify these "deeds of the body" by the Spirit, and then we will live. (Romans 8:13.) Here it is a matter of being a servant of the Spirit. The Spirit will point out our sin – He will lead us to the whole truth and give us the power we need to overcome. If we are faithful and obedient to the Spirit's leading, we get to see and overcome more and more of our sinful human nature as time goes by.

We cannot be more perfect, or serve God more at a given moment, than to the degree that we have received light. But we need to walk in the Spirit, which means acting according to the light that we receive. Then we will get to see more of that flesh, more of that body of sin that is to be destroyed as time goes by. We count ourselves dead to sin (Romans 6:11), so when a new area is revealed to us in God's light, that sin is also crucified. Then we are disciples of Jesus, denying ourselves and taking up our cross daily. (Luke 9:23-24.)

This is a glorious way to walk on! We should not feel bad when God gives us more light and we get to see our sin in this light, but we should rejoice and be happy. Now we can do something about it! Now *we* can put to death the deeds of the body *by* the Spirit. (Romans 8:13; James 1:2-3) It is not the Spirit that does it *for* us; *we* need to do it *by* the Spirit. Then we enter into sanctification – more and more liberation as our body of sin gets destroyed little by little and is replaced by a new creation – the virtues, the life of Christ, divine nature! (Romans 6:5-6; 2 Corinthians 4:10-11; 2 Corinthians 5:17; 2 Peter 1:3-8.)

TO GET LIGHT

*To get light – Getting light means that the Holy Spirit gives you revelation over something. For example, you can get light over your own sin and see that you are selfish, proud, etc. It can also refer to getting more insight (revelation) in the Word of God. (Psalm 119:130.)

GOD HAS GIVEN BELIEVERS THE MINISTRY OF RECONCILIATION

God has given believers the ministry of reconciliation; that is, He uses us to tell the world that they can be reconciled to God through Christ. In this way, we become "Christ's ambassadors, as though God were making his appeal through us" (2 Corinthians 5:20). Verse 19 describes this ministry of reconciliation as proclaiming "the *message* of reconciliation." The message we are to share with the world is this: "Be reconciled to God" (verse 20). We are to tell people of the wonderful opportunity they have to be made right with God through Jesus. We implore them to believe in Christ. Sins do not count against those who are reconciled to God through Christ, because "God made him who had no sin to be sin for us, so that in him we might become the righteousness of God" (verse21).

THIS MINISTRY OF RECONCILIATION IS A BIG RESPONSIBILITY.

This ministry of reconciliation is a big responsibility. God is "making his appeal through us" (2 Corinthians 5:20). The ministry we've been given to turn hearts toward God is urgent and it is vital—it's truly a matter of life and death. Jesus paid the price for our reconciliation because God loves us (John 3:16), so we must share this message of reconciliation in love, and our lives need to reflect our message (Ephesians 4:1). Jesus is the One who saves, and the Holy Spirit is the One who convicts the world of guilt in regard to sin and righteousness and judgment (John 16:8), yet we have been given the privilege of being ambassadors for Christ.

EVERY BELIEVER PLAYS A PART IN THIS MINISTRY OF RECONCILIATION.

Every believer plays a part in this ministry of reconciliation. One plants; one waters, and God brings growth (1 Corinthians 3:7). As we proclaim the gospel, we act as peacemakers, and God blesses such (Matthew 5:9). We tell and live out His message of reconciliation, lives are changed, and God gets the glory.

DO WE BELIEVE THE WORD OF GOD!!!

ALL SCRIPTURE IS GOD-BREATHED [GIVEN BY DIVINE INSPIRATION]

2 Timothy 3:16

Amplified Bible

^{16}All Scripture is God-breathed [given by divine inspiration] and is profitable for instruction, for conviction [of sin], for correction [of error and restoration to obedience], for training in righteousness [learning to live in conformity to God's will, both publicly and privately—behaving honorably with personal integrity and moral courage];

2 Timothy 3:16

King James Version

^{16}All scripture is given by inspiration of God, and is profitable for doctrine, for reproof, for correction, for instruction in righteousness

MATTHEW 4:4

King James Version

^{4}But he answered and said, It is written, Man shall not live by bread alone, but by every word that proceedeth out of the mouth of God.

WHY DID JESUS CHRIST GIVE THE FIVE FOLD MINISTRY?

Walking Worthy (Ephesians 4:1-7)

^{4}I therefore, the prisoner of the Lord, beseech you that ye walk worthy of the vocation wherewith ye are called,

With all lowliness and meekness, with longsuffering, forbearing one another in love;

³Endeavouring to keep the unity of the Spirit in the bond of peace.

⁴There is one body, and one Spirit, even as ye are called in one hope of your calling;

⁵One Lord, one faith, one baptism,

⁶One God and Father of all, who is above all, and through all, and in you all.

⁷But unto every one of us is given grace according to the measure of the gift of Christ.

Christ Descended Into Hell (Ephesians 4:8-10)

⁸Wherefore he saith, When he ascended up on high, he led captivity captive, and gave gifts unto men.

⁹(Now that he ascended, what is it but that he also descended first into the lower parts of the earth?

¹⁰He that descended is the same also that ascended up far above all heavens, that he might fill all things.)

THE FIVE FOLD MINISTRIES AND THE CHRISTIAN NEW CONVERSIAN

(Ephesians 4:8-10)

¹¹And he gave some, apostles; and some, prophets; and some, evangelists; and some, pastors and teachers;

¹²For the perfecting of the saints, for the work of the ministry, for the edifying of the body of Christ:

¹³Till we all come in the unity of the faith, and of the knowledge of the Son of God, unto a perfect man, unto the measure of the stature of the fullness of Christ:

¹⁴That we henceforth be no more children, tossed to and fro, and carried about with every wind of doctrine, by the sleight of men, and cunning craftiness, whereby they lie in wait to deceive;

¹⁵But speaking the truth in love, may grow up into him in all things, which is the head, even Christ:

¹⁶From whom the whole body fitly joined together and compacted by that which every joint supplieth, according to the effectual working in the measure of every part, maketh increase of the body unto the edifying of itself in love.

¹⁷This I say therefore, and testify in the Lord, that ye henceforth walk not as other Gentiles walk, in the vanity of their mind,

¹⁸Having the understanding darkened, being alienated from the life of God through the ignorance that is in them, because of the blindness of their heart:

¹⁹Who being past feeling have given themselves over unto lasciviousness, to work all uncleanness with greediness.

²⁰But ye have not so learned Christ;

²¹If so be that ye have heard him, and have been taught by him, as the truth is in Jesus:

²²That ye put off concerning the former conversation the old man, which is corrupt according to the deceitful lusts;

²³And be renewed in the spirit of your mind;

²⁴And that ye put on the new man, which after God is created in righteousness and true holiness.

²⁵Wherefore putting away lying, speak every man truth with his neighbour: for we are members one of another.

²⁶Be ye angry, and sin not: let not the sun go down upon your wrath:

²⁷Neither give place to the devil.

²⁸Let him that stole steal no more: but rather let him labour, working with his hands the thing which is good, that he may have to give to him that needeth.

²⁹Let no corrupt communication proceed out of your mouth, but that which is good to the use of edifying, that it may minister grace unto the hearers.

³⁰And grieve not the holy Spirit of God, whereby ye are sealed unto the day of redemption.

³¹Let all bitterness, and wrath, and anger, and clamour, and evil speaking, be put away from you, with all malice:

³²And be ye kind one to another, tenderhearted, forgiving one another, even as God for Christ's sake hath forgiven you.

TWO GREATEST COMMANDMENTS

MATTHEW 22:36-40

When a lawyer and expert of the law asked Jesus what the most important commandment is, Jesus responded, "To <u>love the Lord your God with all your heart</u>, with all your soul, and with all your mind...The second is to love your neighbor as yourself."

All of Christianity comes down to how we love God and how everything we do - relationships, work, entertainment, education, displays our love for God. No success, status, or possession will matter at the end of our days. How we loved God and loved others will be our victory.

WE WRESTLE NOT AGAINST FLESH AND BLOOD

<u>Ephesians 6:12</u> *¹²For our struggle is not against flesh and blood, but against the rulers, against the authorities, against the powers of this dark world and against the spiritual forces of evil in the heavenly realms.*

GENERATIONAL SINS

Our families have the greatest influence on our development, including the development of our patterns of sin. Some people even assert that family curses are passed down along generational lines. The belief comes from Old Testament passages which say that God "punishes the children and their children for the sins of the fathers to the third and fourth generation" (<u>Exodus 34:7</u>).

CHAPTER SEVEN

WHO CAN LEGALLY TAKE SATAN TO COURT?

Now let us get started to see if we can legally "TAKE SATAN TO COURT." It may surprise you to know that everyone does not have the legal right to take Satan to the Supreme Court of Heaven. When Jesus Christ ascended into heaven and sat down on the right hand of the Father, He divided humanity into three personality Types, called the Natural, Carnal, and Spiritual Man. The word "Man" is not gender specific but intended by the Bible to mean humanity or mankind both male and female. Every human being can be put into one of these categories. You can easily locate which category you fit in.

Natural Man

1 Corinthians 2:14

14But the natural man receiveth not the things of the Spirit of God: for they are foolishness unto him: neither can he know [them], because they are Spiritually discerned.

The Natural Man "CAN'T LEGALLY" take Satan to the Supreme Court of God because he legally belongs to Satan. Another name for Satan is "devil." Quite the contrary, Satan can take him or her to the Highest Court in Heaven and legally win the case because of the following facts: The Bible tell us that the natural man father is Satan **(John 8:44; 1 John 3:8)**. That the natural man is born in sin and iniquity (Psalms 51:5). Not being able to produce sinless offspring's **(Job 14:4).** Going astray as soon as they are born **(Psalms 58:3).** Having sin issuing from their hearts (Mark 7:19-21). Being wicked and deceitful in their hearts **(Jeremiah 17:9-10).** Having lust of sin **(Romans 6:11-12).** Having sin dwell in them **(Romans 7:5-25).**

The natural man is a totally selfish and corrupted person whether they appear to be or not and only does good when it will benefit them directly. The natural person does not seek the greatest good of all but only the greatest good for themselves. They are stingy with their money, time, talents and abilities. Making money, pleasure and having power seem to be the main focus.

Who Can Legally Take Satan To Court?

Driving force behind living. They do not honor nor truly believe in God. If put in the right environment and push the right buttons the true nature will be manifested.

There is only one way to change this nature and that is to be "Born-Again." Then and only then can he legally Take Satan to Court and win. If you want to know more about being born again, please see chapter ten "You Can Be Part Of The Family Today."

Carnal Man

1 Corinthians 3:1-3

And I, brethren, could not speak unto you as unto spiritual, but as unto carnal, [even] as unto babes in Christ.

² I have fed you with milk, and not with meat: for hitherto ye were not able [to bear it], neither yet now are ye able.

³ For ye are yet carnal: for whereas [there is] among you envying, and strife, and divisions, are ye not carnal, and walk as men?

Romans 8:7-9

⁷ Because the carnal mind [is] enmity against God: for it is not subject to the law of God, neither indeed can be.

⁸ So then they that are in the flesh cannot please God.

⁹ But ye are not in the flesh, but in the Spirit, if so be that the Spirit of God dwell in you. Now if any man have not the Spirit of Christ, he is none of his.

James 4:17

¹⁷Therefore to him that knoweth to do good, and doeth [it] not, to him it is sin.

The carnal man is born-again and has a relationship with God through Jesus Christ but is out of fellowship because of the misuse of human faculties in transgressing the moral law. Theses faculties are not sinful in themselves, but become sinful when used to break the law. The unlawful yieldedness of human faculties to commit sin or "transgressing of the law" **(1 John 3:4)** cause this breach or loss of fellowship.

As a result of this the carnal man "CAN'T LEGALLY" take Satan to Court and win until 1 John 1:9 is obeyed which say, "*If we confess our sins, he is faithful and just to forgive us [our] sins, and to cleanse us from all unrighteousness.*" When this is done in earnest, the breach is healed and fellowship is restored as before. The carnal man suffers from a broken fellowship with the Father and Jesus Christ while in this condition.

This is willful disobedience and Satan has a legal case against him or her. The carnal man is the immature Christian person who is being pulled upward by the spiritual and downward by the natural. The carnal person is constantly compromising what they know to be right and according to the above scripture this leads to sin (James 4:17). They do believe in God and doing right, but is weak. The action, behavior and decision of others control them. They try to wear two faces at the same time, a spiritual and a worldly and neither one fit well. We are told in Matthew 6:24, "*²⁴No man can serve two masters: for either he will hate the one, and love the other; or else he will hold to the one, and despise the other. Ye cannot serve God and mammon."* They are constantly having internal conflicts because of their hypocrisy. The carnal man must do as the scripture says in James 4:7-8, *"Submit yourselves therefore to God. Resist the devil, and he will flee from you. Draw nigh to God, and he will draw nigh to you. Cleanse [your] hands, [ye] sinners; and purify [your] hearts, [ye] double minded."* When you do this you can then take Satan to Court.

I also recommend that the carnal man also read the chapter on "You Can Be Part of The Family Today."

Spiritual Man

1 Corinthians 2:15-16

¹⁵But he that is spiritual judgeth all things, yet he himself is judged of no man.

¹⁶For who hath known the mind of the Lord, that he may instruct him? But we have the mind of Christ.

Who Can Legally Take Satan To Court?

If I have not gotten to you yet, I would like to congratulate you because "YOU ARE THE ONLY ONE WHO CAN LEGALLY TAKE SATAN TO COURT AND WIN." At least for now until we check to see if Satan has any legal rights against you that you have not considered or is not aware of yet. The spiritual man or woman is the mature person and always seeks the greatest good for all, including the environment and all living things therein. They always seek to carry on the work that Jesus left and commanded them to do. They always seek to lift up Jesus and give God the glory in all things. The spiritual Christian is unselfish with their time, money, talents and abilities. The spiritual person is true to God, themselves, and their fellow human being. They do what 2 Timothy 2:15 says, *"¹⁵Study to shew thyself approved unto God, a workman that needeth not to be ashamed, rightly dividing the word of truth."* They seek the face of God through Jesus Christ that they might know their responsibilities to God and their fellowman. God said in James 1:5, *"⁵If any of you lack wisdom, let him ask of God, that giveth to all [men] liberally, and upbraideth not; and it shall be given him."* They seek and are engaged in those activities and worthy causes that will bring love, harmony, and peace to the human race. They are busy keeping the word in James 1:27, "*²⁷Pure religion and undefiled before God and the Father is this, to visit the fatherless and widows in their affliction, [and] to keep himself unspotted from the world.*"

When they do stumble and are deceived by Satan or a lack of knowledge they are quick to exercise 1 John 1:9, to maintain their fellowship with the Lord and the Body of Christ. They understand what the Communion table is all about and their covenant with God through Jesus Christ and the Body of Christ.

Would it surprise you to know that you can do all of this and still be robbed by Satan from receiving your legal blessings that God promised through Jesus Christ? In Ephesians 1:3 it says, "*³Blessed [be] the God and Father of our Lord Jesus Christ, who hath blessed us with all spiritual blessings in heavenly [places] in Christ*". We must do like the scripture says in 1 Peter 5:8-9, "*⁸Be sober, be vigilant; because your adversary the devil, as a roaring lion, walketh about, seeking whom he may devour: ⁹Whom resist stedfast in the faith, knowing that the same afflictions are accomplished in your brethren that are in the world.*"

Please, please do not underestimate Satan believe what Jesus said in John 15:5, "*⁵I am the vine, ye [are] the branches: He that abideth in me, and I in him the same bringeth forth much fruit: for without me ye can do nothing.*" I repeat do not try to handle him yourself, get help from Heaven and "Take Satan to court."

Ok, now you know where you stand and who can legally take Satan to court and why. Next we will look at Satan legal rights giving to him by God that will allow him to kill, steal, and destroy us legally. We will now see if Satan has a legal right against us.

CHAPTER EIGHT

SATAN HAVE LEGAL RIGHTS TOO

If Satan has a legal right to oppress, or torment you "YOU CAN'T TAKE HIM TO COURT AND WIN." Satan will defeat you every time. Satan "CANNOT" torment without a legal right established by God. Satan knows every **"legal"** right God gives him and will absolutely refuse to leave if those rights remain and are not removed by God through forgiveness. In order to take Satan to Court or cast out demons you need to destroy Satan's legal rights over yourself, family, friends, church, community, or what ever you are praying for. Even when sheer strength of the Word of God and persistency forces demons out, if legal rights remain, then demons promptly enter again. Legal rights are sometimes called **"curses."**

SATAN'S LEGAL RIGHTS

As we have said before, the rules are still the same whether you are dealing with an inside case or an outside case. Simply find out what the legal rights are that the demons are using to be able to attach to that person, then get them properly taken care of and broken before the Lord, and then go in there and cast the demons out of that person if they are on the inside of their bodies, or cast them off that person if they are attacking them from the outside of their bodies.

As I had said in the above article, I do not believe that demons can enter in on the inside of a person's body without some type of a specific reason.

I believe that our God is a God of perfect order and reasoning. And if demons are able to get in on the inside of a person's body, then there has to be some kind of specific reason that has allowed this to occur with them. Otherwise, we would all be having demons living on the inside of us 24/7.

Bottom line – demons cannot enter into a person's body without having some kind of legal permission and legal right to be able to do so. They need some kind of an entry point to be able to get in and attach to someone, and that entry point will be their door opener.

There are spiritual laws that are in operation in our world, and even demons have to abide by these spiritual laws that have been set up God. The Bible tells us in Revelation 3:20 that Jesus Himself will stand before us and knock on our doors to see if we will be willing to open up that door and allow Him to come into our lives.

In order to have Jesus come into our lives, we first have to be willing to give Him our direct permission to be able to do so, as God will never force Himself on any of us. He will let us know that He will want to come into our lives and that He will always be knocking on our doors, but we will always be the ones who will decide whether or not we will be willing to open up that door for Jesus to be able to come into our lives.

The reason being is that God has given each one of us a full free will and He will never violate that free will that He has given to each and everyone of us.

And it's the exact same way with demons. Demons cannot enter in on the inside of a person unless they do something specific on their end that will open up the door for them to be able to come into them. And that something specific will be their legal right.

For instance, if someone starts doing heavy drugs or starts to dabble in some area of the occult, and they do not pull out of it within a reasonable length of time, that person's doors could then be opened up as a result of hole now occurring in their protective hedge with the Lord.

And this open door will now allow the demons to be able to come into that person's life and from there, they will either try to get in on the inside of that person's body if they can go that far with it, or they will try and attach to them from the outside, where they will then follow them around like a dark cloud trying to attack them as often as they can from that outside position.

Doing any type of heavy drugs or dabbling with any area of the occult can thus give demons the full legal right to be able to come directly after us, and that is whether we like it or not, or whether we realize it or not.

When demons enter in on the inside of a person's body, they need something specific to feed on. If a person is doing heavy drugs, then what the demons are feeding on is that person's heavy drug usage. If someone is dabbling into witchcraft, then what the demons are feeding on is that person's actual activities in witchcraft.

Deliverance minister Charles Kraft, in his excellent book, "Defeating Dark Angels," says that demons are like rats and they need garbage to feed on.

If you are doing drugs, then the garbage the demons are feeding on is the actual drug usage. And in order to be able to get set free from the demons, you first have to be willing to get rid of the garbage they are feeding on. This means that the person who is doing drugs first has to be willing to give up the drugs before they can get rid of the demons. If they are not willing to give up the drugs, then they will not be able to get rid of the demons who are attached to them.

In order to be able to cast out demons in someone, you first have to take care of and remove their legal rights. If a person is doing drugs, then the drug usage is the legal right that the demons are using to be able to attach to that person.

In order to be able to set this person fully free from the demons who are attached to them, they then have to be willing to go before the Lord in sincere and heartfelt prayer, and confess out their drug usage as a direct sin before Him, and then be willing to repent and renounce this sin, telling God that they will never, ever go back to it again.

Once that person fully confesses and fully repents of their sin before the Lord, then the demons will no longer have any more legal rights to be able to stay attached to that person, and they will then have to leave this person once you start commanding them to leave this person in the name of Jesus.

The garbage will then have been fully removed and they will then have nothing else left to be able to feed from or hang onto.

I want to give you 13 specific areas that will give demons the full legal right to be able to come directly after someone if they happen to fall into any of these specific areas for any extended length of time. Each of these specific areas are major door openers for demons if a person does not pull out of it within a reasonable period of time.

Here are the 13 specific areas that demons will use to come after a person so you can have all of them right at the top of this article. I will then go into each one of these specific areas under the separate captions below so you will know exactly what to look for when dealing with a demonized person.

1. Direct Willful Sin
2. The Occult
3. Inheritance – Generational
4. Unforgiveness
5. Trauma

6. Abuse
7. Ungodly Soul Ties
8. Curses
9. Addictions
10. Fears and Phobias
11. False Religions
12. Cursed Objects
13. Cursed Buildings

Demons are always looking for any of these specific areas to occur with someone, and each one of these specific areas will give demons the full legal right to be able to come directly after someone if they do not pull out of it within a reasonable length of time.

The battle with these demons will either be won or lost on this specific step. Find out what all of their legal rights are with that person, then get all of them properly taken care of and broken with the Lord, and then the demons will have absolutely nothing else left to be able to hold onto.

Their evil grip will have been totally broken off the person with the completion of just this one step alone, and they will then be much easier to cast off the person once you start to directly engage with them in the name of Jesus.

1. Direct Willful Sin

The first thing you will need to look for if a person approaches you for a deliverance from demons is whether or not they have committed any direct willful sins against the Lord.

Obviously not every sin will cause demons to attack us. But where you will get into trouble in this specific area is on the heavier types of sins, especially if those heavier types of sins are being done on some kind of a regular basis for quite a long period of time with no intent by the person to try and pull out of it.

Here are some of the direct willful sins, if committed on any kind of regular basis, will get us into major trouble in the spiritual realm with demons:

1. Any kind of criminal activity
2. Doing any type of heavier drugs
3. Abuse of alcohol
4. Abortion
5. Adultery
6. Inflicting heavy verbal or physical abuse on another person

All of these areas are major door openers for demons. Many people believe that God will turn a blind eye to the sin of fornication.

But if by chance you are fornicating with a partner who has demons attached to them, then you will give full legal rights for the demons to be able to come directly after you if God will allow a hole to occur in the protective hedge that He has set up on you and your life.

Many Christians do not fully realize how serious of a sin this really is with God, as you will still become one flesh with anyone you are fornicating with, even if you are not in love with that person or directly engaged to marry them. You will develop what is called an ungodly soul tie with the person you are fornicating with, and you will then have to fully break that soul tie with the Lord before you will be able to cast the demons off you.

We just recently had several cases come through our site where several women had drawn demons into their bodies as a result of fornicating with men who already had demons attached to them.

Again, this is one sin that should not be taken lightly or taken for granted with the Lord, thinking that He will cut you some slack and prevent any demons from being able to attack you if you decide to directly and willfully disobey His direct Word on this matter.

If the person you are working with has any of these types of specific sins in their background, then what you will have to do to break these kinds of legal rights with the demons is to take the following three steps:

Confess each one of these sins direct to the Lord, apologize to the Lord for engaging in these sins for as long as they have, and then ask God, through the blood of His Son Jesus, to fully forgive them of these sins and to fully wash away the stain of these sins from their souls.

Repent and renounce on each one of these sins. When you repent of a sin, you are telling God that you will never, ever go back to it again. If the person ends up going back to the same sins after they have been delivered from the demons, then the same demons can then come back on them and possibly bring back more demons who are going to be seven times more wicked than the first set of demons were, thus making their next state much worse than what their original state was.

Fully break and fully sever any ungodly soul ties if there were any other partners involved with them in any of the above sin areas.

Again, the Bible very clearly tells us that the wages of sin is always going to be some kind of death. And death in some of these types of sins is going to be demons who will be allowed to attach to that person if they do not pull out of that sin within a reasonable period of time with the Lord.

If the person is not willing to admit that any of the above areas are sins with the Lord, or if they are not willing to repent and pull out of any of these sins, then you will not be able to set this person free from their demons.

The demons will not leave if you try and cast them out because all of their legal rights will still remain fully in place as long as that person refuses to pull out of that specific sin area.

When interviewing the person on any direct willful sins they may have committed against the Lord, also make sure to ask the Holy Spirit to help guide you and show you any other sins that the person may not have realized were direct sins against the Lord.

The more thorough and the more complete you can be when getting this list of legal rights all out on the table, the easier it will be to cast out the demons once you start to directly engage with them.

2. *The Occult*

Another major area to look for is any dabbling whatsoever with any area of the occult. I am talking about playing with a <u>ouija board</u> even one time, or seeing a fortuneteller or psychic even one time.

Just one time with any area of the occult could be a major door opener for demons. I cannot tell you how many emails we have received from people all around the world who have drawn demons into their lives as a result of dabbling or experimenting with different areas of the occult.

And if by chance they have drawn demons into their lives as a result of dabbling with the occult, they will then draw in some of the stronger and more evil types of demons in Satan's kingdom.

This specific sin area is nothing to mess around with. These demons are also the most violent type and the hardest ones to try and actually cast out. They will usually be the ones who will try and fight you tooth and nail before they will leave and pull out of the person.

If the person you are dealing with has any type of occult activity whatsoever in their background, it would be our strong recommendation that you also include this as part of the legal rights to be taken care of with the Lord.

Here is a list of the specific occult activities that you will need to look for when interviewing the person:

1. Fortunetelling – of any kind such as palm reading, crystal ball gazing, numerology, or seeing psychics
2. Tarot Cards
3. Ouija Boards and <u>Automatic Writing</u>
4. Seances and any involvement with mediums or spiritists
5. Astrology and any form of horoscopes

6. I Ching
7. Hypnotism
8. Transcendental Meditation or any type of Far Eastern Meditation
9. Crystals
10. Witchcraft
11. Satanism
12. Voodoo
13. Channeling
14. Reincarnation
15. Astral Projection
16. ESP
17. Dungeons and Dragons – role-playing games
18. New Age Movement techniques and activities
19. Necromancy

Again, any involvement whatsoever with any of the above occult activities should be taken down as a major legal right. Once you have written down all of the occult activities they have ever been involved in, then what you will have to do to properly break this kind of legal right with the Lord is to take the following 4 steps:

Confess this activity out as a direct sin against the Lord and all of His ways. Tell God that you are really sorry for committing this type of direct willful sin against Him, as you have been placing demons ahead of God. People who delve into the occult are actually tapping into demons for supernatural guidance in their lives instead of going direct to the Lord for His guidance in their lives.

Renounce this sin before the Lord, telling God that you will never, ever go back to it again. This sin is so heavy and so serious with the Lord, that you not only have to confess it out as a sin, but you also have to formally renounce it before God, telling Him that you will never dabble or experiment with it ever again.

Burn or throw away all objects associated with the occult. This will include all books, statues, paintings, drawings, notebooks, jewelry, etc. Demons can continue to remain attached to all of these kinds of objects, and if you do not burn or throw all of them away, the demons can continue to remain attached to these objects and thus continue to remain in your house where they can still attack you.

Fully break and sever all ungodly soul ties to any other people they have been closely associated with in the area of the occult they have been dabbling in. Any mentors, teachers, and instructors that have been teaching them can all form out a demonic and ungodly soul tie with them. They have to be willing to fully break away from all of the people they have been associated with in the specific area of the occult they have been delving in.

Again, we cannot emphasize enough how dangerous and deadly this particular legal right is with demons. The number of Christians we have personally seen who have delved into the occult and who have drawn demons into their lives as a result is quite staggering.

3. Inheritance – Generational

Another major area that demons will look to play in is in the area of the family generation line. We have a separate article in our site that will fully explain this particular legal right for you.

You will need to check out the family generation line when interviewing the person to see if there are any curses or any kind of dysfunctional activity going on up their family line that the demons are feeding on and attaching to.

You will need to see if any of their family members have any type of heavier sins on them such as heavy drug abuse, alcoholism, suicide, major depression, any kind of heavy involvement with the occult, or any kind of sexual and/or physical abuse.

If any of their parents or grandparents have demons attached to them as a result of their involvements with these kinds of heavier sins, then what the demons will try and do if they possibly can, is to jump and transfer down the family line, trying to get some of the other members of the family to do the exact same things as their parents and grandparents had been doing.

You Therefore will have some of the children of parents who were abusers and alcoholics become abusers and alcoholics themselves, all as a result of demons transferring down the family generation line trying to get them to do the exact same thing they had been able to get their parents to do.

In the above article, we give you 6 basic steps to break this kind of heavy activity with the demons. I will go ahead and list out 4 of those basic steps in this caption so you can have all of them right at your fingertips.

Confess the sins of your sinning parent to God the Father

Be willing to fully forgive your sinning parent

Break any ungodly soul ties with the sinning parent

Break the curse line of the demons

In the above article on how to break a generational curse line is an actual testimony of a 16-year-old girl who had demons trying to attach to her as a result of the sins of her natural father and grandfather.

We have in this article the exact battle prayer that we had given to her that fully broke the legal rights of the demons who were trying to attach to her. She was able to be set fully free from the demons who were trying to attach to her on the very first attempt with our battle prayer.

4. Unforgiveness

Another major area that demons will really target is in the area of unforgiveness. The reason demons will move in so strongly on this area is due to the following verse:

"^{25}AND WHENEVER YOU STAND PRAYING, if you have anything against anyone, forgive him, that your Father in heaven may also forgive you your trespasses. But if you do not forgive, neither will your Father in heaven forgive your trespasses." (Mark 11:25)

Not only does this verse tell us that God will not be forgiving all of our trespasses if we do not forgive the ones who have trespassed against us, but this verse is also implying that we may have a very hard time in getting any of our personal prayers answered with Him, as it starts out with the specific wording, "And whenever you stand praying."

This phrase could be implying that you may also have a hard time in getting any of your personal prayers answered with God if you are not willing to forgive all of those who have ever trespassed against you in this life. And demons would love nothing better than to be able to shut down your personal prayer life with the Lord.

That is why it is so extremely important that every single Christian do the best they can with the Lord to fully forgive all of those who have ever done them wrong in this life.

<u>Vengeance and payback in this life belongs to the Lord</u>, not to us. There is no reason why any of us should continue to hold onto feelings of anger, bitterness, and hatred towards all of those who have ever harmed us in this life. Sooner or later, all of the people who have ever harmed you in this life will have to face God Almighty Himself for their own personal judgments. And when they do, they will have to answer direct to God for whatever they have done to you in this life.

This is why you can totally let go of all of the people who have ever hurt you in this life into the hands of God, as God will be evening out all of the scores when everything is all finally said and done.

Since this is such a big legal right that demons will use to try and attach to someone, always make sure to delve into this particular legal right when interviewing the person. Find out if they are holding any grudges or any type of unforgiveness towards anyone in their lives. If they are, then lead them in a prayer that will have them totally forgive all of the people who have ever hurt them.

Also tell them that all God is looking for at this time is just for them to make this personal confession out of their mouths direct to Him, even if their feelings and emotions will not be lining up with this confession.

Over a period of time, the Holy Spirit can then move on them to help heal up their emotions from all of the hurts that have been inflicted upon them.

For many people, this will be a real tough request. But the verses from our Bible are so strong and so clear on this issue, that there is simply no room for debate or compromise with the Lord.

Either we forgive others for what they have ever done to us in this life, or the Lord will not be forgiving us of our own trespasses that have been made directly against Him. And that is not a place you want to be in with the Lord in your own personal relationship with Him.

Demons know this and that is why they will do everything they can to try and cause the person to hang onto feelings of bitterness, anger, and hatred towards all of those who have ever hurt them in this life.

That is what the demons will feed on until the person fully releases and fully forgives all of the people for whatever wrongs they have done to them, no matter how bad and how severe those wrongs may have been.

5. Trauma

This next area is one area where many people would not think that demons would be very active on. But do not let this fool you. Examples of trauma in this life where demons will look to fully exploit would be the following types of adverse situations:

The sudden loss of your job

Having to go through a painful and messy divorce

The sudden death of a very close loved one like a spouse or one of your children

A major type of illness

A major car accident where you are seriously injured

Demons will waste no time in trying to move in on these types of extreme situations. How many times do we see reported in our daily news that someone has just killed his wife due to a pending divorce, or someone has killed several people at the job where they had just been laid off at.

The sudden loss of a job, the breakup of a marriage, or the sudden death of your spouse or one of your own children can all cause severe depression to sink in very quickly.

And from there, that person could very easily sink into a heavy pit of despair where they are no longer wanting to live anymore. Some of these types of situations will cause some people to literally take their own lives, as they cannot handle the grief, despair, and anguish they are going through.

When demons see these kinds of extreme situations unfolding before them, they will then move in to try and push that person right over the edge of the cliff, trying to get them to either commit suicide, or try to get them to kill the other people that are associated with the pain they are now feeling – like the fellow employees at the job they just got laid off at, or the spouse who is filing for a divorce against them.

Spirits of fear, rejection, and depression will be some of the main demons who will then try and move in on a situation like this. The shock and trauma of a major event like some of the ones described above can break down a person's normal defenses and thus create a big opening for demons to be able to move in to try work the situation to their advantage.

The remedy for this type of extreme situation is the full surrender, which we have listed as one of the main steps in being able to receive a full deliverance from the Lord. Bottom line – lead this person into a full surrender and explain to them that God will now start to move and guide them out of whatever adverse situation they may have just fallen into.

If they have just lost their job, God can now move to lead them to the next job that He will want them to have. If they have been involved in a bad car accident, God can now move to heal them up and start to help guide them through all of the things they will need to do to properly resolve everything.

If a person has just lost a close loved one in a sudden death, God can help comfort them and help bring them peace and explain to them that they will be reunited with their loved one once they leave this life and enter into heaven.

If someone is going through a painful and messy divorce, God can still move to give them a brand new start and a brand new life if for whatever reason He did not move earlier on to keep the marriage together.

Bottom line – whatever adverse situation you may end up facing in this life, it will not be the end of the world for you.

If God can create our entire world in 6 days, then He can also help you handle any type of adverse situation you may have just fallen into, no matter how bad and how hopeless things may appear to you in the natural.

If nothing is impossible with God, then He will have no problems in being able to help you handle whatever adverse situation may have just struck you with the force of a tornado.

If you suspect that demons are trying to attach to someone as a result of them going through some type of traumatic event, then lead that person into a full surrender prayer where they will now turn their entire problems and their entire lives over into the hands of God the Father for Him to fully handle. Once you do that, then the demons will no longer have any more legal rights to hang onto, as they will know now that God will be in full control over everything from this point on.

Once they do that full surrender prayer to the Lord, then He will move in to take full and complete control over every detail in their lives, including helping them handle whatever adverse situation that may have just come into their lives.

Once that full surrender has been made to the Lord, then you can directly engage with the demons, telling them to back off and that they no longer have any more legal claim over this person since they have just made that full surrender to the Lord.

6. Abuse

Another major area to always look for with demons is any kind of abuse in the person's background. This would include any kind of sexual abuse. Any kind of heavy verbal and/or physical abuse. Demons will try to move in very quickly on both the abuser and the ones they are abusing if they see any kind of verbal, physical, and sexual abuse being inflicted upon someone for any appreciable length of time.

If there is any abuse in the person's background with any of their parents, boyfriends, or spouses, it would be our strong recommendation to also include this as a valid legal right and then go ahead and properly break it before the Lord.

What you will have to do to properly break this kind of legal right is to take the following two steps:

1. Forgive all of the people who have ever abused them in their past.
2. Fully break and sever any ungodly soul ties that have developed between the person and the people who have abused them, even if it is one or both of their parents.

Again, God will just be looking for a confession out of their mouths at this stage when they are trying to forgive all of those who have ever abused them, even if their emotions and feelings are not lining up with the confession that will be coming out of their mouths.

Over a period of time, the Holy Spirit can then move down into their emotions and start the inner healing process so their emotions can eventually come into line with their right thinking on this matter. But you do not have to wait for all of this to occur before you can cast out the demons.

As long as they are in complete agreement with you and they are willing to make a complete, formal confession out of their mouths to the Lord that they will be willing to forgive all of the people who have ever abused them, that will then be good enough with the Lord, and you can then move to cast the demons out of them after they have fully forgiven everyone.

7. Ungodly Soul Ties

As you can see from some of the above legal rights, the issue of soul ties will come up quite frequently with many of these legal rights. This should be another area that you automatically check when interviewing the person, since this one is such a frequent legal right that the demons will use.

A soul tie can either be a good one or a bad one. A good soul tie is when you develop a good, godly, and healthy spiritual bond with another person. Good soul ties should be developing between parents and their children, between husbands and wives, and between people who are good friends with one another.

A good example of a good type of soul tie in the Bible is the friendship that had occurred between King David and Jonathan. The Bible says that the souls of David and Jonathan were knitted together. Here is the verse:

"¹And it was so, when he had finished speaking to Saul, that the soul of Jonathan was knit to the soul of David, and Jonathan loved him as his own soul." (1 Samuel 18:1)

But just as a soul tie can be a good, godly, and healthy one, they can also go in the opposite direction where they can then become ungodly and unhealthy. This happens quite a bit in heavy abuse type situations, where the abuser is trying to control and manipulate the one they are abusing.

Once this starts to occur, the one who is being abused will start to fear the one who is abusing them and they will then do everything they can to try and please the abuser so the abuse will be kept at minimum levels.

But this obviously never works. Once this cycle of abuse starts to occur, the abuser never lets up and they will then continue on with the abuse until the person has had enough and decides to break away from that person.

However, with all of the abuse this person has taken over the years, there is always the possibility that demons will move in to try and attach to the person who is being abused.

If the person does not break away from the one who is abusing them within a reasonable length of time, then an ungodly soul tie could develop between the two of them. As such, it would be our recommendation to also include this as a possible legal right.

Ungodly soul ties can also occur between parents and their children if the parents are abusing their children. It can also occur between a husband and wife if the one spouse is either verbally and/or physically abusing the other spouse. Ungodly soul ties can also occur between two friends if the one starts to try and control and manipulate the other one against their own will.

God has given each man and each women a full free will and no one has the right to violate that free will that has been given to us by God. We should always respect one another's free will and not try and force our wishes or our ways on another person.

Not even God Himself will violate our free will. He will always give us the ability and the freedom to make our own choices in this life, even if many of those choices will end up being the wrong choices for our lives.

If God Himself gives us the ability to make free will choices in our lives, then so should the other people who in our lives. But yet so many people in this life like to try to control and manipulate others for their own gain and profit.

As a result, many people fall into slavery to other people because they are too afraid to stand up for themselves and too afraid to try and break away from the ones who are abusing them. Since demons are all about control and domination, they will waste no time in moving in on someone if they see they are being abnormally controlled and manipulated by another person.

As such, every unhealthy and ungodly soul tie that is still in a person's life needs to be fully broken before the Lord so the demons will have nothing else left to feed on and attach too.

8. Curses

There are 3 types of curses that demons can use to come after someone.

A) *Direct Curses* – this is where someone who is heavy into the occult will try and curse someone direct. Both witches and Satanists will try and do this with those who they think are their enemies, and we as Christians are definitely one of their direct enemies.

However, our Bible tells us that a curse cannot land on us without a cause. In other words, if a witch or a Satanist tries to send a curse our way, it will not land on us due to the protection that we already have with God. But if we have done something that would have caused a hole to occur in our protective hedge with the Lord, then that curse might be able to get through and land on us. And if it does, then the demons who will be attached to that curse will then try and attack us.

Here is the verse from our Bible telling us that a direct curse cannot land on us without some type of proper cause being in place:

"²Like a flitting sparrow, like a flying swallow, so a curse without cause shall not alight." (Proverbs 26:2)

If the person you are working with tells you that a curse has already been sent their way by someone who is into the occult, and they are already under direct attack from the demons who are riding on that curse, then the first thing you will need to determine is if this person has done anything on their end that would have caused a hole to occur in their protective hedge with the Lord.

If the person has done something sinful to have caused a hole to occur in their protective hedge with the Lord, then get it properly taken care of and broken with the Lord. Then once you do that, you can then form out the appropriate battle prayer to break the curse and the hold that it still has on this person.

For instance, if this person was also dabbling in the occult, then they will have to break this legal right like we explained above under the occult caption.

Then once that person has both fully confessed and fully renounced their sin of being involved in the occult before the Lord, then they can turn around and directly engage with the curse and the demons who are riding on it and render it completely null and void in the name of Jesus.

If by chance they have not done anything that would have caused a hole to occur in their protective hedge with the Lord, then you can have them directly engage with the demons, telling them that this curse has no cause to be able to land on them, and that you will now prevent this curse from being able to harm them any further.

You can also plead the blood of Jesus directly against the curse, directly against the person who is sending the curse their way, directly against the demons who are riding on this curse, along with pleading the blood directly around them so as to form out a protective covering and shield for them.

B) *Self- Cursing* – the next type of curse that can come someone's way is when a person actually curses their own selves. Good examples of self-cursing are when someone is constantly telling themselves that they are no good, they will never amount to anything, they will never achieve any of their goals or dreams, they are too fat and ugly, they will never have any true friends, or that no one is ever going to like them, approve of them, or love them.

This type of negative thinking can really do damage to one's self-esteem and self confidence. And from there, it can prevent that person from ever being able to reach their true divine destiny and their true potential in the Lord in this lifetime.

The Bible tells us that we are transformed by the renewing of our minds, and part of that renewal process is getting the right type of thinking put into our minds and thought process.

When you are constantly talking down to yourself, you are in fact cursing your own self with your own words. When demons see someone who is constantly doing this and they are making no attempt to pull out of it, they will waste no time in moving in to help that person out even more.

The demons will then interject their thoughts into the person's mind, telling them that they are in full agreement with their own destructive words to themselves, that they really are a nobody, that no one will ever love them, that they are a total failure in this life, and that they will never amount to anything good or worthwhile in this life.

What the demons will try and do is to keep the pressure on from their end so they can either try to get this person to commit suicide, or throw them into a severe state of depression where they will no longer be able to function in this life anymore.

If the person you are dealing with has demons attached to them as a result of a lot of self-cursing on their end, then what you will have to do before you can cast the demons off them, is to get their thinking straightened out in the Lord.

Tell them and show them who they really are in Jesus Christ. Tell them that God has a specific plan, purpose, and calling for their lives. Tell them that God is no respecter of persons and that He loves them and cares for them as much as He does anyone else.

Once you get their thinking half-way straightened out, then you can go after the demons, telling them that they no longer have any more legal rights to this person now that this person has been told what the real truth is and who they really are in Jesus Christ.

C) General Curses – these are non-deliberate types of curses. Examples of these types of curses are when someone close to you makes a cutting and hurtful remark, like you will never make it if you try and go to college, or don't try to become a doctor because you are not smart enough, etc.

We can all remember specific hurtful words that we have received from our parents or close friends that had cut right through us like a knife and have stayed with us for quite a long period of time. But again, you have to remember that God is in total control of your life, not your parents or your close friends.

God will decide what He will be wanting you to do for him in this life, and nothing can alter that divine course that has already been set up for your life by the Lord but yourself.

Hurtful words from any of your parents and close friends will not alter your divine destiny with the Lord unless you allow it to do so. In other words, do not believe and keep dwelling on any type of hurtful type words when they do come your way, no matter who they may come from.

Jeremiah 29:11-29

¹¹For I know the plans I have for you," declares the Lord, "plans to prosper you and not to harm you, **plans** *to give you hope and a future. (C) ¹²Then you will call (D) on me and come and pray (E) to me, and I will listen (F) to you. ¹³You will seek me and find me when you seek me with all your heart.*

Just realize that we are all imperfect and every once in awhile people will say mean and hurtful things to you. But do not take what they say to heart – and do not let it get a foothold into your mind and thought process.

If you do, it can then curse you and from there, you can start to believe and act on it. And once you start to believe and act on it, demons could then move in to try and make your situation even worse.

They will just add more lies to the ones already spoken out to you, and before you know it, you will have fallen into a state of depression and despair, thinking that your life is now over and not even God can help you now.

If the person you are working with has any of this type of wrong thinking in their minds, again, build them up in the Word and let them know who they really are in Jesus.

Tell them that Jesus already has a perfect divine plan set out for their lives and for them to learn how to let the Holy Spirit straighten out their thinking. Once you get them built up a bit in the Word on this issue, then cast the demons off them, as they will then lose their evil grip on the person once that person starts to get their thinking lined up with the way that God will want them to be thinking in this life.

These last two types of curses really do show us how powerful spoken words can be when they are released to other people or even to our own selves. We can literally curse other people and even our own selves without really meaning to do so.

Once again, the Bible really hits the nail on the head when it tells us that we all carry either life and death in our tongues – and it is up to each and every one of us as to what kinds of words we will release to the other people who are in our lives. Too many people are bringing death, cursing, and misfortune to other people with what is coming out of their mouths, especially to those who are very close to them.

9. Addictions

This next legal right is also a major feeding ground for demons. You can break addictions down into two different types – those that are behaviorally based and those that are chemically based. But whether an addiction is chemically based or behaviorally based, once again, demons will waste no time in moving in to try and make matters even worse.

Here are some of the specific addictions that demons will try and move in on if person does not try and pull out if it within a reasonable amount of time:

- Alcohol
- Cocaine
- Heroin
- Meth
- Marijuana
- LSD
- Anti-prescription drugs
- Anorexia
- Bulimia
- Gluttony

To be set free from both the demons and the addictions that are on them, the person has to be willing to take the following three steps:

Confess out the addiction as a sin before the Lord and ask Him to fully forgive them and wash away the stain of this sin from their soul and body.

Ask God, by the power of the Holy Spirit, to take out this addiction from their personalities and lifestyle if they do not have enough will power on their own to pull out of it. The will need an inner healing from the Holy Spirit.

Once they have fully surrendered their addictions over to the Lord for His full and complete handling, then engage with the demons, telling them that they no longer have any more legal rights to stay attached to this person since they will now be under God's direct authority and power from this point on – and that they will now be working very closely with the Holy Spirit to remove this addiction and stronghold from their life.

If the person is really bound up and they do not think they can break free from their addictive lifestyle, show them from the Word that there is nothing that God cannot do, including being able to set them fully free from whatever they are addicted to.

Explain to them that as a Christian, they already have the Holy Spirit residing on the inside of them, along with His full divine power to be able to set them fully free from both their specific addictions and the demons who are attached to them.

10. Fears and Phobias

With the mind being the actual battlefield in the area of spiritual warfare, demons will always look for any sign of abnormal, mental weakness. And this is where you get into some of the different types of abnormal fears and phobias that people can develop.

These types of fears and phobias are all irrational. The normal person will not have these types of irrational fears operating on them. Examples of these types of irrational fears are the following:

Being too afraid to drive again if they have been involved in a car accident.

Women being too afraid of men if they have been sexually abused in their past. This type of unhealthy fear will also prevent them from ever being able to have a normal healthy relationship with another man.

Fear of failure if they have always been told by their parents and friends that they will never amount to anything. This type of irrational and unhealthy fear can also keep them from being able to reach what God has called them to do for Him in this life.

Initially, all of these types of irrational fears are totally understandable at the outset if they have come into a person's life as a result of some kind of abuse or trauma. But where people can get into trouble in this realm is if they wallow too long in these types of unhealthy fears.

If they do not get a proper grip on this type of unhealthy fear, this fear can then take over their entire life where they will no longer be able to function in certain areas of their lives as a result of that fear always hounding and following them. And from there, demons can then move in to intensify the fears they are already feeling.

If a woman has been sexually abused by her father during part of her growing years in the household, then she could have a very hard time in being able to trust any man when she gets out on her own, as she will always think and feel that every man that she will ever meet will be just like her father.

If she does not pull out of this type of irrational fear within a reasonable period of time, that fear could then cripple and paralyze her and prevent her from ever being able to marry anyone, thus causing her to miss out on a real big blessing that God would have wanted her to have in this life. And this was all as a direct result of an abnormal and irrational type of fear totally controlling and dictating her life.

Demons know that these types of irrational fears and phobias can totally shut someone down in the Lord, so again, they will waste no time in moving in to try and make matters even worse for the person.

Once spirits of fear and paranoia attach to this kind of person, they will then become even more bound up than what they already were, and before you know it, they won't trust anyone in their lives.

To help set this kind of person free from both their fears and the demons who are attached to them, they will need to take the following 2 steps:

Confess out their fears to the Lord, asking Him to take complete control of their thought life and emotional life and ask Him, by the power of the Holy Spirit, to do inner surgery on them so they can get their thinking straightened out and their emotions healed up so their irrational fears do not continue to rule over them and destroy their lives. They will have to make a full and complete surrender of their bodies, their souls, their spirits, and their entire lives over to the Lord so that He will be fully free to start the inner healing process with them.

Once that full surrender has been made to the Lord, along with a request for His direct help in getting them cleaned up and healed from their irrational fears – then directly engage with the demons, telling them that they no longer have any more legal rights to stay attached to this person now that they have turned the reigns of their entire lives over to the Lord, along with asking for His direct help in taking out these types of abnormal and irrational fears that have been operating in them for too long of a period of time.

After this kind of heartfelt prayer is made to the Lord, then the Holy Spirit will start to move to take out these kinds of irrational fears and phobias the person may have developed over the years from any kind of dysfunctional activity or traumatic events they may have experienced.

11. False Religions

We believe there is only one way to God the Father and His kingdom of heaven, and that is only through His Son Jesus Christ and His sacrificial death on the cross. We do not believe there are any other names or any other ways into the kingdom of heaven other than through Jesus Christ and His sacrificial death on the cross.

As such, every other false religion that is out there has been set up by Satan and his demons. If you are dealing with a person who has come from any of these other false religions, you will first have to be able to convert them over to Jesus. If they are not willing to accept Jesus Christ as their true Lord and Savior, then you will not be able to set them free from the demons who are attached to them.

If they are willing to accept Jesus Christ as their true Lord and Savior, then what you will have to do with them, if by chance they have demons attached to them as a result of being involved in a false religion or cult, is the following:

Have them formally renounce their allegiance to the previous false religion or cult they had been involved in.

Then directly engage with the demons, telling them that this person is now a brand new creation in Jesus Christ, that they now belong to Him and Him alone, and that all of their legal rights have now been fully removed and fully broken since they have now fully renounced all ties and all allegiances to the false religion they had been previously involved in.

Once the person fully renounces all ties and allegiances to the false religion or cult they had been previously involved in, then the demons will no longer have any further legal rights to this person, and they will then have to leave this person once you start to command them to leave in the name of Jesus Christ.

12. Cursed Objects

Another major area where demons like to play in is with cursed objects. Demons can literally attach themselves to certain types of objects. And if a person happens to bring one of these cursed objects into their house, the demons can then start to attack the people who are living in the house as a result of them being attached to that object.

The legal right they are now using will be the cursed object itself. That is why in the above caption on the occult that we have you immediately discard every single object that is associated with the occult in any way.

Here is a very good verse from our Bible that is telling us that we are not to bring cursed objects into our houses:

"25You shall burned the carved images of their gods with fire; you shall not covet the silver or gold that is on them, nor take it for yourselves, lest you be snared by it; for it is an abomination to the Lord your God. Nor shall you bring an abomination to the Lord your God. 26Nor shall you bring an abomination into your house, lest you be doomed to destruction like it; but you shall utterly detest it and utterly abhor it, for it is an accursed thing. "(Deuteronomy 7:25-26).

Another area where people can get into trouble is when they go overseas and bring back objects from other pagan nations. Bringing back any kind of a statue, painting, drawing, or jewelry of a foreign god from a pagan nation can also become a major entry point for demons to be able to enter into your house.

If demons are attached to the object that you have just brought back home and you allow it to stay in your house, the demons will then be able to set up shop in your house and start to attack the various members of your family.

If by chance the person you are working with has demons roaming in their house as a result of them being attached to a particular object they have brought back home with them, have them take the following 3 steps:

Go before God and confess this out as a sin before Him, telling Him that you are sorry and that you did not know that this particular object was cursed with the presence of demons on it.

Burn or throw away this cursed object so it is fully removed from their house.

Then do a full house cleansing.

What you will want to do when doing a full house cleansing is to walk around the perimeter of the house claiming both the house and the land for the Lord, pleading the blood of Jesus around the house so that no further demons can try and get back in, anoint the main rooms of the house with anointed oil over the top of the entrances, and then cast out any evil spirits that might still be trying to hang on, telling them that all of their legal rights have now been fully removed with the discarding of the cursed objects they were all attached to.

13. Cursed Buildings

Another area where people can come under direct demonic attack is when they move into a new house that already has demons in there from the previous owners. If the previous owners were involved in any kind of occult activity, and they then leave and sell the house to the next set of owners, the demons who were attached to the previous owner can still stay in that house due to the legal rights that were granted to them by the previous owner.

This means that the new owners of the house will have to do a full house cleansing when they move in. Again, the new owners should walk around the perimeter of the house claiming both the land and the house for the Lord. Then plead the blood of Jesus around both the house and the land so they can have God's full protection over all of their property.

From there, anoint each one of the main rooms in the house by applying anointed oil over the tops of the entrances into each one of the rooms, once more claiming each of the rooms for the Lord and commanding any demons who are still in there to now leave in the name of Jesus Christ.

When doing the house cleansing, also tell the demons that you are now the new home owners, that you have not given them any legal rights to be able to attach to you, and that they will now have to leave your new house since you had no involvement whatsoever with the previous owners or whatever else they were involved in that gave them the legal rights to be able to stay in the house in the first place.

I would also have the person try to find out what the previous owners were involved in that allowed the demons to attach to the house in the first place. If you can find out what the specific legal rights were from the previous owner, you can then use that additional information in your prayer once you start to do the house cleansing.

Conclusion

When trying to help someone who has demons attached to them, whether those demons be on the outside of their bodies or living on the inside of their bodies, the above 13 areas will give you a good place to start so you can find out exactly what the legal rights are that is allowing these demons to still continue to remain attached to this person.

When interviewing the demonized person, just make a list of every single major legal right that you can uncover as you question them on their past.

Then once you have all of the legal rights written down on paper, then form out the appropriate type of prayer to have all of these legal rights properly taken care of and broken with the Lord. You will also have to break each one of these legal rights individually with the Lord.

And then once you have fully broken all of their legal rights with the appropriate kind of prayer to the Lord, then you can go directly after the demons, telling them that all of their legal rights have now been fully broken and that they will now have to leave this person in the name of Jesus.

There are many kinds of "**Curses**" but, they can be divided into the following categories, I will not discuss each curse at this time but will only list them:

Iniquity, Abominations, Spirit Guides, Tattoos, Unforgiveness, Soul Ties, Psychic Heredity, Names given by ancestors and others

Occult, Satyr, Strange Religions, Vows and Dedications, Roman Catholicism, The Passive Mind (Meditations), Holistic Healing, Sexual Curses, Hexes, and Religious and Cultural ties (Traditions).

Curses of Iniquity

Exodus 34:6

⁶And the LORD passed by before him, and proclaimed, The LORD, The LORD God, merciful and gracious, longsuffering, and abundant in goodness and truth,

⁷Keeping mercy for thousands, forgiving iniquity and transgression and sin, and that will by no means clear [the guilty]; visiting the iniquity of the fathers upon the children, and upon the children's children, unto the third and to the fourth [generation].

The same is found in Exodus 20:5:

Exodus 20:5

⁵Thou shalt not bow down thyself to them, nor serve them: for I the LORD thy God [am] a jealous God, visiting the iniquity of the fathers upon the children unto the third and fourth [generation] of them that hate me;

⁶And shewing mercy unto thousands of them that love me, and keep my commandments.

Also in Duteronomy 5:9:

⁹Thou shalt not bow down thyself unto them, nor serve them: for I the LORD thy God [am] a jealous God, visiting the iniquity of the fathers upon the children unto the third and fourth [generation] of them that hate me.

Also in Numbers 14:18-20:

Numbers 14:18-20

¹⁸The LORD [is] longsuffering, and of great mercy, forgiving iniquity and transgression, and by no means clearing [the guilty], visiting the iniquity of the fathers upon the children unto the third and fourth [generation].

¹⁹Pardon, I beseech thee, the iniquity of this people according unto the greatness of thy mercy, and as thou hast forgiven this people, from Egypt even until now.

²⁰And the LORD said, I have pardoned according to thy word.

Deuteronomy 18:9-12

⁹When thou art come into the land which the LORD thy God giveth thee, thou shalt not learn to do after the abominations of those nations.

¹⁰There shall not be found among you [any one] that maketh his son or his daughter to pass through the fire, [or] that useth divination, [or] an observer of times, or an enchanter, or a witch,

¹¹Or a charmer, or a consulter with familiar spirits, or a wizard, or a necromancer.

¹²For all that do these things [are] an abomination unto the LORD: and because of these abominations the LORD thy God doth drive them out from before thee.

God Has Not Changed His Mind

God has not changed His mind about these curses caused by sin. In Heb. 13:8 it says that, *"Jesus Christ the same yesterday, and to day, and for ever."* You may be thinking that Jesus did not give these curses because they are given in the Old Testament. But, I will remind you that it says in John 14:9, *"Jesus saith unto him, Have I been so long time with you, and yet hast thou not known me, Philip? he that hath seen me hath seen the Father; and how sayest thou [then], Shew us the Father?"*

There is still no amnesty, or statue of limitation for sin except repentance by the Blood of Jesus. It says in Proverbs 28:13, *"He that covereth his sins shall not prosper: but whoso confesseth and forsaketh [them] shall have mercy."* These words are still just as powerful, potent and true today as they were then. Sin is still an abomination before God today and all the curses listed below are still in effect today.

New Testament Example

In John 9:2-3 it says, *"And his disciples asked him, saying, Master, who did sin, this man, or his parents, that he was born blind? Jesus answered, Neither hath this man sinned, nor his parents: but that the works of God should be made manifest in him."* The disciples believed that the man was born blind because the parents of the man had caused him to be under a generational curse. But, Jesus corrected them and said that this man was born blind so that the power of God could be demonstrated over the power of Satan. This was still under the Old Testament but Jesus came to destroy the works of the devil (1 John 3:8).

In the Old Testament it says in Lev. 20:11, *"And the man that lieth with his father's wife hath uncovered his father's nakedness: both of them shall surely be put to death; their blood [shall be] upon them."* This was an Old Testament Law that God commanded to be carried out. Capital punishment was the sentence for such a crime. Both of them were put to death.

In the New Testament the same crime was committed and this is what Paul said about it. In 1 Cor. 5:1-5 it says, *"It is reported commonly [that there is] fornication among you, and such fornication as is not so much as named among the Gentiles, that one should have his father's wife. And ye are puffed up, and have not rather mourned, that he that hath done this deed might be taken away from among you. For I verily, as absent in body, but present in spirit, have judged already, as though I were present, [concerning] him that hath so done this deed, In the name of our Lord Jesus Christ, when ye are gathered together, and my spirit, with the power of our Lord Jesus Christ, To deliver such an one unto Satan for the destruction of the flesh, that the spirit may be saved in the day of the Lord Jesus."*

Even though this man was saved Satan was giving a legal right to put cancer or whatever he wanted to use to bring this Christian to an early death. So you see these curses are still in effect today. The method may have changed because they no longer stone people.

Our modern culture may not believe this is wrong but God looks at it as a capital crime and give Satan a legal right to cause death unless it is repented of and forgiven by God through Jesus Christ. God will have the last and final Word.

The Sexual Curse of Our Modern Times

Very few families possess "**clean**" ancestries, untainted by any occultic involvement or idolatry. One sin in particular, illegitimacy, brings curses down even unto the tenth generation (Deut. 23:2). "*Illegitimacy*" also called a "*bastard*" is the state of being born of unwed parents. This sin is very prevalent in our modern society of sexual freedom. In fact, many people young and old are not even aware of this curse upon their lives. Even so called Christians are having sex out of wedlock and coming under this curse. Notice that most of the curses move through the family lines for two or three generation but notice the importance that God puts on this curse. **This sin brings curses down even unto the tenth generation:**

Deuteronomy 23:2

2 A bastard shall not enter into the congregation of the LORD; even to his tenth generation shall he not enter into the congregation of the LORD.

Many saints suffer torments, misfortune, accidents, and poverty without knowing why. This includes practicing Christians who love God, tithe on a regular basis, read their Bibles daily, and attends church three times a week. Yet they unknowingly live under a curse sent down the generation's lines. Many are tormented by occultic spirits because their ancestors practiced witchcraft, fortune telling, or other occultic activity as mentioned above.

Biblical Curses

Sins bring curses. **Proverbs 26:2** says, "*As the bird by wandering, as the swallow by flying, so the curse causeless shall not come.*" We are discussing curses, which have been pronounced by God not hexes that comes from witches and other people.

Curses Allowed By God:

Those who curse or mistreat Jews (**Gen. 12:3; Num. 24:9**).

Against willing deceivers (**Josh. 9:22-23; Jer. 48:10; Mal. 1:14; Gen. 27:12**).

On adulterous women **(Num. 5:27)**.

Disobedience to the Lord's commandments **(Deut. 11:28; Dan. 9:11; Jer. 11:3)**.

Idolatry **(Jer. 44:8; Deut. 29:18-20; Exod. 20:5; Deut. 5:8-9)**.

Those who keep or own cursed objects **(Deut. 7:25; Josh. 6:18)**.

Refusing to come to the Lord's help **(Judg. 5:23)**.

House of the wicked **(Prov. 3:33)**.

Refusing to give to the poor **(Prov. 28:27)**.

The earth, because of man's disobedience **(Isa. 24:3-6)**.

Jerusalem is a curse to all nations if Jews rebel against God **(Jer. 26:4-6)**.

Thieves and those who swear falsely by the Lord's name **(Zach. 5:4)**.

Ministers who fail to give the glory to God **(Mal. 2:1-2)**.

Those who rob God of tithes and offerings **(Mal. 3:8-9)**.

Those who hearken unto their wives rather than God **(Gen. 3:17)**.

Those who dishonor their parents **(Deut. 27:16)**.

Those who create graven images **(Deut. 27:15)**.

Those who willfully cheat people out of their properties **(Deut. 27:17)**.

Those who take advantage of blind people **(Deut. 27:18)**.

Those who oppress strangers, widows, or fatherless **(Deut. 27:19; Exod. 22:22-24)**.

He who lies with any beast **(Deut. 27:21; Exod. 22:19)**.

He who lies with his sister (incest) **(Deut. 27:22)**.

Those who smite their neighbors secretly **(Deut. 27:24)**.

Those who take money to slay the innocent **(Deut. 27:24)**.

Adulterers **(Deut. 22:22-27; Job 24:15-18)**.

The proud **(Ps. 119:21)**.

Those who trust in man and not the Lord **(Jer. 17:5)**.

Those who do the work of the Lord deceitfully **(Jer. 48:10)**.

Those who keep back the sword from blood **(Jer. 48:10; 1 Kings 20:35-42)**.

Those who reward evil for good **(Prov. 17:13)**.

Murderers **(Exod. 21:12)**.

Those who murder deliberately **(Exod. 21:14)**.

Children who strike their parents **(Exod. 21:15)**.

Kidnappers **(Exod. 21:16; Deut. 24:7)**.

Those who curse their parents **(Exod. 21:17)**.

Those who cause the unborn to die **(Exod. 21:22-23)**.

Those who do not prevent death **(Exod. 21:29)**.

Witchcraft practitioners **(Exod. 22:18)**.

Those who sacrifice to fake gods **(Exod. 22:20)**.

Those who attempt to turn anyone away from the Lord **(Deut. 13:6-18)**.

Those who follow horoscopes (astrology) **(Deut. 17:2-5)**.

Those who rebel against pastors and leaders **(Deut. 17:12)**.

False prophets **(Deut. 18:19-22)**.

Women who keep not their virginity until they are married **(Deut. 22:13-21)**.

Parents, who do not discipline their children, but honor them above God **(1 Sam. 2:27-36)**.

Those who curse their rulers **(Exod. 22:28; 1 Kings 2:8-9)**.

Those who teach rebellion against the Lord **(Jer. 28:16-17)**.

Those who refuse to warn sinners **(Ezek. 3:18-21)**.

Those who defile the Sabbath **(Exod. 31:14; Num. 15:32-36)**.

Those who sacrifice human beings **(Lev. 20:2)**.

Participants in seances and fortune-telling **(Lev. 20:6)**

Those involved in homosexual lesbian relationships **(Lev. 20:13).**

Necromancers and fortune telling **(Lev. 20-27).**

Those who blaspheme the Lord's name **(Lev. 24:15-16).**

Those who are carnally minded **(Rom. 8:6).**

Those who practice sodomy **(Gen. 19:5-15, 24-25).**

Rebellious children **(Deut. 21:18-21).**

Are There Curses In your Mouth?

Someone once said if we wanted to know the causes of all our problems, frustrations, and failures, we need not look any further than two inches below our nose and there we will find our "mouth." The Word of God says in **Psalms 139:14,** that we are *"fearfully and wonderfully made...."* God has made us in His image according to **Gen. 1:26.** God spoke the world into existence by saying what He wanted to happen with His mouth **(Gen. 1:3).** When God created man in His image, He created another "speaking spirit." Just like God he could call those things which be not as though they were **(Rom. 4:17).**

Since Satan got control of man's mouth and tong he has been speaking curses against himself, God, his fellowman, and the environment. He has been cursing everything in seen and unseen. Read James chapter three. The following scriptures in Proverbs reveal how important our "mouth" and "tong" is in blessing and cursing others and ourselves. Verses **18:21** tell us that *"death and life are in the power of the tong..."*; **6:2** says, *"Thou art snared with the words of thy mouth, thou art taken with the words of thy mouth."*; **10:11** says, *"the mouth of a righteous [man is] a well of life; but violence covereth the mouth of the wicked;"* **Verse 12:14** says, *"A man shall be satisfied with good by the fruit of [his] mouth, but the soul of the transgressors [shall eat] violence;"* **Verse 13:3** says, *"He that keepeth his mouth keepeth his life: [but] he that openeth wide his lips shall have destruction;"* **Verse 15:4** says, *"A wholesome tongue [is] a tree of life: but perverseness therein [is] a breach in the spirit."* There are many,

many more scriptures that prove my point. Read how Jesus cursed the fig tree with His mouth in **Mark 11:11-14; 20-24.** Jesus did this to teach His disciples **"the power of the tong."**

There is a direct connection with your mouth and the course of your life. Your mouth and the quantity and quality of your life. Your mouth determines your destiny. Your mouth determines your failure or success, pleasure and pain, victory or defeat, blessings and cursing. We might be giving Satan many legal rights to destroy our lives and our loved ones every day, instead of working with Jesus to deliver and give us victory and "salvation" over Satan. It says in Proverbs 16:25, *"There is a way that seemeth right unto a man, but the end thereof [are] the ways of death."*

Have you ever spoken words of cursing to yourself or others like these?

"You are no good."

"You will never amount to anything."

"You will be dead or in jail before you are such and such age."

"God will never answer my prayers."

"I can't do anything right."

"I am always sick."

"I feel like dying."

"That just kills me."

"You make me sick."

"I always catch the flu every year."

"Nothing good ever happens to me."

"I am so stupid,"

"You are so stupid!"

"You worry me to death."

"God damn this or that."

"The corona-virus will kill me sooner or later."

We are told in Col.3:8, "*⁸But now ye also put off all these; anger, wrath, malice, blasphemy, filth communication out of your mouth.*" We are also commanded in Col.3:17, "*¹⁷And whatsoever ye do in word or deed, [do] all in the name of the Lord Jesus, giving thanks to God and the Father by him.*" Speaking words like the one above gives Satan legal right over us.

Sin leads to curses. Accordingly, if a person continues to live in sin, deliverance will either not be possible, or happen only temporarily.

Many Christians unwittingly bring abominations into the home such as:

Statues of the Virgin Mary, Different Saints, Tarot cards, Kwan Yin, Buddha, Shiva, Carvings of tiki gods, voodoo dolls, Books on the occult, Fortune telling, Stones and rocks from heathen temples, Paintings of Romans and other gods, I-Ching books, Ceramic and macramé depictions of frogs, owls, dragons, Rock-and-roll records, Dungeon and Dragon games, Good-luck oriental dolls, Samurai swords (the real kind), Martial arts magic words (called "hus"), Buddhist altars, Aztec carvings, use of Ouija boards, Souvenirs manufactured by Hare Krishna followers have all been the sources of curses Seemingly innocent objects have been manufactured by Buddhists and strange religions who pray over their products and "bless" them. If you are involved in any of this or such like, "YOU CAN'T TAKE SATAN TO COURT." and win. Read **Acts 19:19**. Well-meaning friends pin good-luck charms on children or give away occultic crystals and wind chimes that are actually objects of Hindu, Buddhist, or Taoist worship.

Jewelry and other demonic objects are often found in Christian homes, posing as art objects and decorations. These cursed things bring strange diseases that doctors cannot diagnose, divorces, rebellious children, arguments, accidents, and oppression.

Demons will not leave until the cursed objects are taken out of the house or destroyed.

LGBT ON THE RISE

LGBT history dates **back to the first recorded instances of same-sex love and sexuality of ancient civilizations, involving the history of lesbian, gay, bisexual, and transgender (LGBT) peoples and cultures around the world.** What survives after many centuries of persecution—resulting in shame, suppression, and secrecy—has only in more recent decades been pursued and interwoven into the culture.

The number of people identifying as transgender is on the rise in the United States of America and the United Kingdom, including many children and teens. This year the American Academy of Pediatrics published findings that more teenagers are beginning to use "non-traditional gender terms" to self-identify.

One man's journey from deception to truth
by Stephen Black

February 1, 2019

Sex became a distorted issue for me at an early age. I was molested about age 6 by a male friend of the family who was babysitting me. I was also exposed to some pornography at the same time. The porn was heterosexual, but it was devastating to my understanding of real love and God's design for sexuality.

At age 7, I was again exposed to pornography. One of my brother's friends was reading an article about testing yourself to see if you might have homosexual tendencies. The article asked in very explicit ways if you were attracted to men or women.

My mind was reeling from the pictures and the feelings that I was having. Then the older boy showed the pictures to me and asked, "Who would you kiss, the man or the woman?"

I became frightened, convinced that I was going to get in trouble. I remember wanting to answer what I thought he wanted to hear. *Well, we are all boys*, I thought, *and little boys are not supposed to be interested in girls.* So I told him, "The man."

My brother's friends all laughed and repeated over and over, "You homosexual, you queer." Their voices of ridicule rang in my mind for days.

Several years later, our next-door neighbors had some out-of-state visitors. I was playing at their house and was followed into the garage by the adult male visitor. He molested me while warning me to keep quiet.

About a year later, my family went on a trip to Colorado. We stayed with friends who had a son several years older than me. That night, I was molested again. A year later, he came to visit at my house and it happened again.

When I was 12, I switched from a private Catholic school to public school and soon was introduced to drugs. I started smoking marijuana and listening to hard rock music. I totally rejected what little I knew of God. I became sexually active with a girl from school and surrounded myself with peers who encouraged me to continue in sin.

About a year later, I went into a deep depression as a result of being bullied and beat up by school peers. The depression worsened, as I kept having homosexual thoughts, desires and dreams. My family and friends became very concerned. One night I decided to kill myself. I probably would have succeeded if a friend hadn't come over. He correctly guessed my struggle—then told me he was bisexual and that it was perfectly normal. A false peace settled over me as I realized that one of my closest friends understood my struggles.

I broke off my relationship with my girlfriend and pursued a relationship with this male friend. As I went through high school, I met homosexual men and started going to gay bars. Soon I had a new goal: to be "married" to another man.

"I knelt beside my bed and cried out to God for forgiveness. I asked Jesus to totally change me. It was Feb. 6 1983, and my new life had begun."

Over the following years, I pursued a marriage-type relationship with several men. I had one relationship that lasted two years. One of these men, Mike, was wealthy, and we lived in a beautiful home.

Mike introduced me to a priest, who told me that being homosexual was OK with God. "God created us this way," he said, "and He loves us just the way we are."

Still, I became depressed again for several months, and I cried out to God, asking Him to show me the truth about being gay.

My relationship with Mike ended in a horrible fight. Before long, I became sexually involved with another man, and then with a woman who was trying to help me out of homosexuality. But being involved in heterosexual sin carried just as much guilt for me.

Then I got a phone call from Mary, an old high school friend. She took me to visit her sister, who was "real religious." Several people were there, and they talked about Jesus in a familiar way that I had never heard before.

Suddenly I had an overwhelming feeling that I needed to accept Christ that night. My heart started pounding.

I turned to a man named Steve and said, "I need to know Jesus like you do." We prayed together, and I received Jesus Christ into my life.

Later that night, I went to my bedroom with the old family Bible and prayed for God to show me where homosexuality was wrong. I opened the Bible, came to Leviticus chapter 18, and my eyes fell upon verse 22: "You shall not lie with a male as one lies with a female; it is an abomination." I knelt beside my bed and cried out to God for forgiveness. I asked Jesus to totally change me. It was Feb. 6, 1983, and my new life had begun. I have never been the same.

The Lord led me to a church where people really loved Him. My supervisor at work asked his prayer group at the church to begin praying for me.

I told him that I had been gay. "Jesus can change your life if you submit totally to Him," he told me. His in-laws were so excited to hear that I'd become a Christian that they invited me to live with them while I became established as a new believer. I stayed with them for the next year.

I began meeting weekly with my pastor, who helped me to deal with the underlying root issues of my homosexual struggles, such as lust, anger, unforgiveness and the sexual abuse I had experienced as a child. When the anger and bitterness came pouring out, several men and women in my church prayed with me and ministered God's healing to my broken heart.

After I had been a Christian for over a year, I began thinking about marriage. "God," I prayed, "if You want me to be married, You will have to bring a woman into my life who loves You as much as I do!"

Some months later, Robin began attending my church. We became friends and were married on May 25, 1986. We have a very fulfilling marriage and enjoyed raising three children (Robin had one daughter when we married, whom I adopted as my own). All our children are now adults and married, and we have three grandchildren. Our youngest daughter went to be with Jesus unexpectedly at age 21 as a result of complications from a brain mass.

From my own experience, I know that deliverance from homosexuality comes only through a new lifestyle of absolute surrender, completely depending upon the Lord Jesus Christ while processing a history of abuse and pain. God's blessings never cease when we are open to Him, walking in obedience to His will. ©2019 Stephen Black

POWER AGAINST SEXUAL PERVERSION

Romans 6:14

Sexual sins open the doors for all kinds of evil spirits to enter, this prayer progamme is for those:

Who would like to be delivered from the spiritual contamination resulting from past sexual sins.

Who would like to be delivered from their present sexual lusts, enticement, and other sexual sins.

Who would like to expel sexual satanic deposits acquired by sleeping with demonised people.

Who had been a commercial sex worker in the past.

Who frequently dream of having sex.

Don't despair if the enemy has subjected you to such a depth of immoral degradation. You would be lifted up to the height of purity which God has purposed for you as you call upon him to help you.

Rom. 1:22: *"²²Professing themselves to be wise, they became fools."*

Please, open your Bible and slowly, meditatively read **Rom. 1:18- 32** and **Leviticus 18:1-30**. Are u surprised at the things you've just read? Indeed, there is nothing new under the sun! **(Ecclesiastes 1:9)**

Basically the laws of God concerning sexual perversion as stated in **Leviticus 18** can be divided into 5 groups. They are laws against:

incest (I.e having sex with close relatives, brothers, in law's uncles etc., there are 20 categories of close relatives stated between verses 6 & 19) adultery (vs 20)- idolatry I.e.

Offering child sacrifices (vs21) homosexuality, lesbianism, masturbation, prostitution etc (VS 22) bestiality (having sex with animals (vs 23)

Are you caught in the bondage of any of these? Indeed, the chains of habit (perversion) are two weak to be felt till they are too strong to be broken. All kinds of sexual bondage can be broken through the power of the blood of Jesus. There is hope for you, the Bible says, "Sin shall not have dominion over you" **(Rom. 6:14)** because, "The law of Spirit of life in Christ Jesus has set you free from the law of sin and death" **(Rom 8:2)**

As you pray sincerely with a contrite/repentant heart **(Psalm 51:17)** God will set you free from the chains of sexual perversion.

CONFESSION

Gal. 5:24: *24And they that are Christ's have crucified the flesh with the affections and lusts.*

PRAISE WORSHIP

1. Thank God for his power to deliver from every bondage.
2. I break myself from every spirit of sexual perversion, in the name of Jesus.
3. I release myself from every spiritual pollution emanating from my past sins of fornication and sexual immorality, in Jesus' name.
4. I release myself from every ancestral pollution, in the name of Jesus.
5. I release myself from every dream pollution, in the name of Jesus.
6. I command every evil plantation of sexual perversion in my life to come out with all its roots, in the name of Jesus.
7. Every spirit of sexual perversion working against my life, be paralyzed and get out of my life, in the name of Jesus.
8. Every demon of sexual perversion assigned to my life, be bound, in the name of Jesus.
9. Father Lord, let the power of sexual perversion oppressing my life receive the fire of God and be roasted, in the name of Jesus.
10. Every inherited demon of sexual perversion in my life, receive the arrows of fire and remain permanently bound, in the name of Jesus.
11. I command every power of sexual perversion to come against itself, in the name of Jesus.
12. Father Lord, let every demonic stronghold built in my life by the spirit of sexual perversion be pulled down, in the name of Jesus.

13. Let every power of sexual perversion that has consumed my life be shattered to pieces, in the name of Jesus.

14. Let my soul be delivered from the forces of sexual perversion, in the name of Jesus.

15. Let the Lord God of Elijah, arise with a strong spirit wife/husband and all the powers of sexual perversion, in the name of Jesus.

16. I break the hold of any evil power over my life, in Jesus' name.

17. I nullify every effect of the bite of sexual perversion upon my life, in the name of Jesus.

18. Every evil stranger and all satanic deposits in my life, I command you to be paralyzed and to get out of my life, in the name of Jesus.

19. Holy Ghost fire, purge my life completely, in the name of Jesus.

20. I claim my deliverance from the spirit of fornication and sexual immorality, in the name of Jesus.

21. Let my eyes be delivered from lust, in the name of Jesus.

22. As from today, let my eyes be controlled by the Holy Spirit, in the name of Jesus.

23. Holy Ghost fire, fall upon my eyes and burn to ashes every evil force and all satanic power controlling my eyes, in Jesus' name.

24. I move from bondage to liberty in every area of my life, in the name of Jesus.

25. Thank God for answers to your prayers.

Other Curses To Consider

I will only mention briefly a few other curses to consider, that will cause you "Not To Take Satan To Court":

(1) The curse of flying off the handle

The curse of flying off the handle is the curse of uncontrolled emotions. Giving someone a piece of your mind and letting people know when they have gotten on your last nerve. Having a bad attitude and showing negative emotions such as anger, hate, resentment, jealousy, envy and such like.

Unforgiveness

The word of God says in Mark 11:26, *"²⁶But if ye do not forgive, neither will your Father which is in heaven forgive your trespasses."* This verse speaks "Loud and Clear" for itself. If you don't forgive God, others or yourself, it is futile to even try to take Satan to court.

(3) Disobedience

The Word of God says in 1 Sam. 15:22, *"...²²Behold, to obey [is] better than sacrifice..."* If you don't repent of your sins don't try it. It says in James 4:17, *"¹⁷Therefore to him that knoweth to do good, and doeth [it] not, to him it is sin."* Willful disobedience brings curses upon you.

Preparing To Take Satan To Court

Breaking Curses

Galatians 3:13

¹³Christ hath redeemed us from the curse of the law, being made a curse for us: for it is written, Cursed [is] every one that hangeth on a tree.

I break every curse that gives Satan a legal right in my life to keep me from receiving the material and spiritual blessings that God has for me through Jesus Christ.

Our Father, I come by the precious blood of our Savior Jesus Christ. I stand on the Word of God in Galations 3:13. Christ has redeemed me from the curse of the law, having served as a curse for me. For it is written, Cursed is everyone who hangs from a tree. I thank you, Lord Jesus, for serving as a curse for me, and I now claim your precious Blood to take away all curses. By the authority given to me by God, I break the following curses: Illegitimacy, Poverty, pride, witchcraft, etc.

(Immediately following a reading and breaking of those curses, call out the demon spirits.)

In the name of Jesus, and by the power of His blood, I command you to come out and leave. You, spirit of cancer, diabetes, poverty, pride, sexual lust, witchcraft etc., come out! Spirit of lust, you come out in Jesus name.

Go down the list of spirits. At first, the spirits may be stubborn and not manifest, but be as stubborn and persistent as they are. They must come out. Believe the Word of God that says in **James 4:7-8**, "*⁷Submit yourselves therefore to God. Resist the devil, and he will flee from you. ⁸Draw nigh to God, and he will draw nigh to you. Cleanse [your] hands, [ye] sinners; and purify [your] hearts, [ye] double minded.*"

Ask God to reveal to you the curses that you are under. Make sure that all known sins are confessed and forsaken. We read in Proverbs 28:13, "*He that covereth his sins shall not prosper: but whoso confesseth and forsaketh [them] shall have mercy.*

TAKE SATAN TO COURT!!!!

CHAPTER NINE

SATAN IS A PROSECUTOR AND JESUS CHRIST IS OUR DEFENSE ATTORNEY

The word "devil" comes from the Greek word *diábolos*, which means "accuser."

We Have Connections in Heaven

Romans 8:1

"[There is] therefore now no condemnation to them which are in Christ Jesus, who walk not after the flesh, but after the Spirit."

If you have passed all the previous tests and you still believe you have a legal right to take Satan to Court, the next step is to get some spiritual warfare knowledge. Satan can still defeat you without this knowledge. The Word of God says in Hosea 4:6, "⁶*My people are destroyed for lack of knowledge: because thou hast rejected knowledge, I will also reject thee, that thou shalt be no priest to me: seeing thou hast forgotten the law of thy God, I will also forget thy children.*" You must know that you have a legal right to approach God to present your case. You must know what Jesus Christ is doing for you "**NOW IN HEAVEN,**" and know your "**COVENANT RIGHTS.**" The blood of Abraham sealed the First Covenant, and God sacrificed an animal as a substitute. This New Covenant is sealed with the blood of Jesus Christ, God's own Son.

In Heb. 8:1 it says, "*We have such a high priest, who sat down on the right hand of the throne of the Majesty in the heavens.*" Jesus is the minister of the true tabernacle, which the Lord prepared instead of Moses. Everything that we do centers around our New High Priest Jesus Christ under the New Covenant, but our High Priest can never fail His people.

In Heb 8:6 it says, "*⁶But now hath He [Jesus] obtained a ministry the more excellent, by so much as He is also the Mediator of a better covenant which hath been enacted upon better promises.*"

The High Priest was an earthly mediator between Israel and Jehovah. Jesus is the Mediator of the New Covenant between God and us.

Exploring The Book of Hebrews

The book of Hebrews has several vital contrasts. There is the contrast of:

Moses and Jesus.

Aaron, the High Priest, and Jesus the New High Priest.

The blood of bulls and goats and the blood of Christ.

The two tabernacles, the one reared by Moses and the one in Heaven.

Into the tabernacle in Heaven went Jesus and sat down there as our High Priest. His home is the Holy of Holies. The Priest under the Old Covenant could only stay long enough to make the Atonement. **Heb. 9:21-23** tells how the tabernacle and all the vessels were cleansed with blood.

Hebrews 9:21-23

²¹Moreover he sprinkled with blood both the tabernacle, and all the vessels of the ministry.

²²*And almost all things are by the law purged with blood; and without shedding of blood is no remission.*

²³*[It was] therefore necessary that the patterns of things in the heavens should be purified with these; but the heavenly things themselves with better sacrifices than these.*

This is a startling thing, that Adam's sin had touched heaven itself. The twentieth fourth verse says,

Hebrews 9:24

²⁴*For Christ is not entered into the holy places made with hands, [which are] the figures of the true; but into heaven itself, now to appear in the presence of God for us.*

This is the climax of it all. This let us see the contrast of God's estimation of the blood of Christ and the blood of bulls and goats. As we come to value the blood of Christ as God values it, then the problem of our standing and relationship never enters our minds.

Christ The New Mediator

The blood of bulls and goats, under the first Covenant, only cleansed or sanctified the flesh, but the blood of Christ is to **"cleanse our conscience from dead works," so that we may stand uncondemned in the presence of the living God.**

Because God accepted Jesus' blood when He carried it into the Heavenly Holy of Holies, He has become by that act the Mediator of the New Covenant.

John 20:17

¹⁷*Jesus saith unto her, Touch me not; for I am not yet ascended to my Father: but go to my brethren, and say unto them, I ascend unto my Father, and your Father; and [to] my God, and your God."*

1 Timothy 2:5

⁵*For [there is] one God, and one mediator between God and men, the man Christ Jesus."*

The reason man needs a mediator is because he has lost his standing with God. He has no ground on which he can approach

God. Therefore, he can't plead his case before the Supreme Court of God. Natural man is really an outlaw. Eph. 2:12 describes his sad condition:

Ephesians 2:12

¹²That at that time ye were without Christ, being aliens from the commonwealth of Israel, and strangers from the covenants of promise, having no hope, and without God in the world."

Jesus is now to be the Mediator between God and fallen man. The blood of bulls and goats did not take away sin, it merely covered it temporarily. But when Christ came, He Redeemed all of those who had trusted in the blood of bulls and goats. **"He died for the redemption of the transgressions that were under the first covenant."**

Those sacrifices, under the old covenant, were like a promissory note, which He cashed on Calvary. God kept His covenant with Israel when He sent His Son to become sin, and He laid upon Him all the sins under the First Covenant, that by accepting Him as their Savior Israel might come into the promised Redemption.

Jesus Completely Put Sin Away

This is the great heart teaching of the book of Hebrews. Under the First Covenant sin was "**covered.**" The best that the Israelite had under the First Covenant was a blood covering or Atonement. You remember the word "**Atonement**" means, "**to cover.**" This presented a fearful situation every year, because everything centered around the High Priest under the Old Covenant. When the High Priest failed, the people had neither approach nor mediator between them and God. This condition brought awesome fear to the people from year to year.

But praise God, under the New Covenant our sins are not "**covered,**" They are put away. They are "**remitted.**" They are wiped out as though they had never been, according to (Rom. 8:1). The word "**remission**" is never used but in connection with the "**New Birth.**" When we come to Jesus Christ as a sinner, and take Christ as Savior, confess Him as our Lord, then all that we have ever done is wiped out. We only need to be concerned about the sins that we commit from that point on. Then we have (**1 John 1:9**) to take care of those. Because of Jesus Christ, in the New Birth all that we have ever been stops being and a New Creation takes the place of the old (**2 Cor. 5:17**). **Heb. 9:25- 26** says,

²⁵Nor yet that he should offer himself often, as the high priest entereth into the holy place every year with blood of others;

²⁶For then must he often have suffered since the foundation of the world: but now once in the end of the world hath he appeared to put away sin by the sacrifice of himself.

The expression "**end of the ages**" really means where the two ages met. The cross was where the old method of counting ended (**Dispensation of Law**), and it was the place where the new time began (**Dispensation of Grace**). The thing that stood between man and God was Adam's transgression. Jesus "**Put That Away**" and gave us a standing before God that we did not have before.

2 Corinthians 5:21

²¹For he hath made him [to be] sin for us, who knew no sin; that we might be made the righteousness of God in him.

Jesus settled the sin problem, made it possible for God to legally remit all that we have ever done, and give to us Eternal Life, making us New Creations.

2 Corinthians 5:17

¹⁷Therefore if any man [be] in Christ, [he is] a new creature: old things are passed away; behold, all things are become new.

¹⁸And all things [are] of God, who hath reconciled us to himself by Jesus Christ, and hath given to us the ministry of reconciliation.

Jesus Christ The One Sacrifice

The changing of the Covenant and the changing of the Priesthood left Israel almost homeless. To leave the gorgeous temple for street preaching, in groves and cottages was an innovation that almost staggers ones mind. The one sacrifice that Jesus made ended the slaughtering of animals, the carrying of blood into the Holy of Holies. It was the end of sin covering

Hebrews 1:3

³Who being the brightness of [his] glory, and the express image of his person, and upholding all things by the word of his power, when he had by himself purged our sins, sat down on the right hand of the Majesty on high.

This **"once for all"** offering ended the scapegoats bearing away sin.

We must read **Lev. 16:1-22** carefully in order to get the picture of the great day of Atonement and the scapegoat.

This was the annual day of humiliation and expiation for the sins of the nation, when the high priest made the atonement for the sanctuary, the priests, and the people. The high priest, laying aside his official ornaments, first offered a sin-offering for himself and for the priesthood, entering into the Holy of Holies with the blood. He afterward took two he-goats for the nation. One was slain for Jehovah. On the head of the other the sins of the people were typically laid; it was made the sin bearer of the nation; and laden with guilt, it was sent away into the wilderness.

Mark 15:38 tells of the death of Jesus and the rending of the veil between the Holy place and the Holy of Holies where the blood was carried and sprinkled upon the Mercy Seat.

Mark 15:38

³⁸And the veil of the temple was rent in twain from the top to the bottom. This was the end of the Holy of Holies on earth. It was the beginning of a New Covenant in His Blood. Acts 20:28 tells us that this was the blood of God.

Acts 20:28

²⁸Take heed therefore unto yourselves, and to all the flock, over the which the Holy Ghost hath made you overseers, to feed the church of God, which he hath purchased with his own blood.

Heb. 9:12, He had carried this blood of Deity into the Holy of Holies in the New Tabernacle, not made with hands, in the heavens.

Hebrews 9:12

¹²Neither by the blood of goats and calves, but by his own blood he entered in once into the holy place, having obtained eternal redemption [for us].

It was what He called the "once for all" sacrifice.

Christ Ministry Today

Most Christians have neglected the present ministry of Christ. So many, when they think of His giving His life for us think only of His death and Resurrection.

They do not know that when He sat down on the Father's right hand, that He began to live for us in as much reality as He had died for us. He is no longer the lowly man of Galilee. He is not the Son made Sin for us, forsaken of God. He is the Lord of all. He has conquered Satan, sin, and disease. He has conquered death. He possesses all authority in Heaven and in earth.

Matthew 28:18

¹⁸And Jesus came and spake unto them, saying, All power is given unto me in heaven and in earth

We can act fearlessly upon His Word, because He stands back of it. He is the Surety of it. He is the Surety of this New Covenant.

Hebrews 7:22

²²By so much was Jesus made a surety of a better testament.

Jesus Christ Is Our High Priest

The High Priest of the Old Covenant was a type of Christ, the High Priest of the New Covenant is "**Christ Himself**." Once every year the High Priest under the Old Covenant had entered into the tabernacle on earth with the blood of bulls and goats to make a yearly atonement for the sins of Israel.

Hebrews 9:25

²⁵Nor yet that he should offer himself often, as the high priest entereth into the holy place every year with blood of others.

Hebrews 10:1-4

¹For the law having a shadow of good things to come, [and] not the very image of the things, can never with those sacrifices which they offered year by year continually make the comers thereunto perfect.

²For then would they not have ceased to be offered? because that the worshippers once purged should have had no more conscience of sins.

³But in those [sacrifices there is] a remembrance again [made] of sins every year.

⁴For [it is] not possible that the blood of bulls and of goats should take away sins.

The priests stood daily, ministering and offering the same sacrifices for the sins of Israel **OVER and OVER**. Those sacrifices could never take away sins.

Hebrews 10:11

¹¹And every priest standeth daily ministering and offering oftentimes the same sacrifices, which can never take away sins.

Christ entered into Heaven itself with His own blood, having obtained eternal redemption for us. **CHRIST DID IT ONLY ONCE.**

<u>When God accepted the blood of Jesus Christ, He signified that the claims of Justice had been met, and that man could be legally taken from Satan's authority and restored to fellowship with Himself.</u>

By the sacrifice of Himself, Christ had put sin away. By the sacrifice of Himself, He had sanctified man. **To sanctify means to "set apart," "to separate."** <u>**He had separated man from Satan's kingdom and family.**</u>

When Christ met Mary after His Resurrection, (John 20:17) He said to her, **"Touch me not, for I am not yet ascended unto the Father."**

He was then on His way to the Father with His own blood, the token of the penalty He had paid, and human hands could not touch him.

Jesus' ministry as High Priest did not end with His carrying His blood into the Holy Place, but He is still the minister of the Sanctuary. Heb. 8:2.

The word, "Sanctuary" in the Greek means "Holy things."

He is ministering in the "Holy Things." These "Holy Things" are our prayers and worship.

We do not always know how to worship Him [God] as we ought, but He takes our crude petitions and worship and make them beautiful to the Father.

Every prayer, every worship is accepted by the Father when it is presented in the Name of Jesus.

He is a merciful and faithful High Priest. He can be touched with the feelings of our infirmities. **Heb. 4:14-16.**

Hebrews 4:14-16

14 Seeing then that we have a great high priest, that is passed into the heavens, Jesus the Son of God, let us hold fast [our] profession.

15 For we have not an high priest which cannot be touched with the feeling of our infirmities; but was in all points tempted like as [we are, yet] without sin.

16 Let us therefore come boldly unto the throne of grace, that we may obtain mercy, and find grace to help in time of need.

He is High Priest forever.

Hebrews 6:19

19 Which [hope] we have as an anchor of the soul, both sure and stedfast, and which entereth into that within the veil;

Jesus Christ Our Mediator

When Christ sat down at the Father's right hand, He had satisfied the claims of Justice, and He became the Mediator between God and man.

Jesus is man's mediator for two reasons: because of what He is, and because of what He has done.

First, Jesus is man's mediator by virtue of what He is. He is the union of God and man. He is the one who existed on an equality with God, made in the likeness of men.

Philippians 2:8-9

⁸And being found in fashion as a man, he humbled himself, and became obedient unto death, even the death of the cross.

⁹Wherefore God also hath highly exalted him, and given him a name which is above every name.

Hallelujah!!! He has bridged the gulf between God and man. He is equal with God, and He is equal with man. He can represent humanity before God. This however, was not a sufficient ground for a mediation between God and man. Man was an eternal criminal before God and needed to be reconciled back to Him. Man was alienated from God, and under the judgment of Satan.

Second, Jesus is man's mediator because of what He has done. **Col. 1:21-22** says,

Colossians 1:21-22

²¹And you, that were sometime alienated and enemies in [your] mind by wicked works, yet now hath he reconciled

²²In the body of his flesh through death, to present you holy and unblameable and unreproveable in his sight.

2 Corinthians 5:18

¹⁸And all things [are] of God, who hath reconciled us to himself by Jesus Christ, and hath given to us the ministry of reconciliation.

There could have been no mediator between God and man if there had not been first a Reconciliation made between God and man.

Man was unrighteous in His condition of spiritual death. While he was in that condition, He could not approach God. Neither could any Mediator have approached God for him. Satan had every human being in his grip and man could not free himself.

Christ has reconciled us unto God through His death on the cross, so that He now presents man holy and without blemish before God. **Therefore, man has a legal right to approach God through Christ, his mediator. I can now take Satan to court.**

From the fall of man until Jesus sat down at God's right hand, no man had ever approached God except over a bleeding sacrifice, through a Divinely appointed priesthood, or by an angelic visitation or dream.

On the ground of His High Priestly offering of His own blood, He perfected our Redemption, He satisfied the claims of justice and made it possible for God to legally give man Eternal Life, making him righteous, and giving him a standing as **Sons and Daughters.**

He is the Mediator of the New Covenant.

Hebrews 9:15

¹⁵And for this cause he is the mediator of the new testament, that by means of death, for the redemption of the transgressions [that were] under the first testament, they which are called might receive the promise of eternal inheritance.

Jesus is seated at the right hand of the Father. **He is the High Priestly Mediator that is to introduce lost men to God.**

Man has no approach now but through the new Mediator. By one sacrifice He has put sin away, and by one act He carried His blood into the Holy of Holies.

By that one act Heb. 10:19 declares that all can now enter boldly through the veil into the very presence of the Father and stand there without condemnation.

Hebrews 10:19

¹⁹Having therefore, brethren, boldness to enter into the holiest by the blood of Jesus,

I pray that we are able to make the church understand this blessed truth. There is so much sin-consciousness, and so little consciousness of the Finished work of Jesus Christ taught. We hear Him cry in, **Heb. 4:14-16,**

Hebrews 4:14-16

¹⁴Seeing then that we have a great high priest, that is passed into the heavens, Jesus the Son of God, let us hold fast [our] profession.

¹⁵For we have not an high priest which cannot be touched with the feeling of our infirmities; but was in all points tempted like as [we are, yet] without sin.

¹⁶Let us therefore come boldly unto the throne of grace, that we may obtain mercy, and find grace to help in time of need.

We hear **His LOUD CRY SAY, "Come boldly to the throne of grace and find a blessing to meet every need."**

It seems to me as though the Master were saying, "Stop your crying, stop your groaning, come with joy to the throne of love and get back what Satan has stolen from you."**Take Satan To The Supreme Court of Heaven."**

Heb. 10:12-13 tells us that one sacrifice of His own blood now in the presence of the Father, on the Mercy Seat, has made all this available to those who take Christ as Savior and Lord.

His work is finished. In the Father's mind our Redemption is complete. Satan does not have any power over us anymore. We belong to God through Jesus Christ.

Jesus Christ Our Intercessor

Romans 8:34

³⁴Who [is] he that condemneth? [It is] Christ that died, yea rather, that is risen again, who is even at the right hand of God, who also maketh intercession for us.

Hebrews 7:25

²⁵Wherefore he is able also to save them to the uttermost that come unto God by him, seeing he ever liveth to make intercession for them.

Jesus, as High Priest, carried His blood into the Holy of Holies, satisfying the claims of Justice that were against natural man.

As Mediator, He introduces the unsaved man to God. John 14:6, Jesus is the way to God, and no one can approach God except through Him. As soon as man accepts Christ he becomes a child of God. Then Christ begins His intercessory work for him.

Jesus is Mediator for the sinner, but He is intercessor for the Christian.

The first question that comes to us is: "Why does the child of God need someone to intercede for him?

We can find the answer to that in **Rom. 12:2.**

Romans 12:2

²And be not conformed to this world: but be ye transformed by the renewing of your mind, that ye may prove what [is] that good, and acceptable, and perfect, will of God.

At the New Birth, our spirits receives the life of God. The next need is that our minds be renewed.

Before we came into the Family, we walked as natural men... Satan ruled men. Satan ruled our minds. Now that our spirits have received the life of God, our minds must be renewed so that we will know our privileges and responsibilities as children of God.

The New Birth is instantaneous, but the renewing of our mind is a gradual process. Its growth is determined by our study and meditation on the Word.

During this period we need the intercession of Christ. Many times we strain our fellowship with the Father, as in our ignorance of His will, we many times say and do things that are pleasing to Him.

Then again, we need His intercession because of demonic persecution against us. Demons persecute us for righteousness sake. They hate and fear us because God has declared us righteous. Because we have not fully learned of our authority they cause us to stumble many times.

Regardless of this, He is able to save us to the uttermost, because He ever lives to pray for us.

Hebrews 7:25

25 Wherefore he is able also to save them to the uttermost that come unto God by him, seeing he ever liveth to make intercession for them.

No one can lay anything to the charge of God's child. God has declared him righteous. There is no one to condemn him. Jesus is living to make intercession for him.

Therefore when Satan come against us to steal, kill or destroy we have a legal right to take him to court.

Romans 8:33-34

33 Who shall lay any thing to the charge of God's elect? [It is] God that justifieth.

34 Who [is] he that condemneth? [It is] Christ that died, yea rather, that i risen again, who is even at the right hand of God, who also maketh intercession for us.

Jesus Christ Is Our DEFENSE ATTORNEY

We came to the Father through Christ, our Mediator. We have felt the sweet influence of His Intercession on our behalf. Now we want to know Him as our Advocate before the Father. We need Jesus to plead our case before the Father the Righteous Judge when we take Satan to court. Jesus has never lost a case and you can be sure that He want loose our when we have a legal right to bring Satan to court.

Many Christians today, who are living in broken fellowship, would be living victorious lives in Christ if they knew that Jesus was their advocate.

Because of our unrenewed minds and Satanic persecution, we sometimes sin and cause our fellowship with the Father to be broken.

Every child of God who breaks fellowship with the Father is under condemnation. If he had no advocate to plead his case before the Father he would be in a sad position.

The word shows us that if we do sin we have an advocate with the Father.

Consider the meaning of the word "advocate." In Webster's dictionary we read: "One who defends, vindicates, or espouses a cause by argument; an upholder; a defender; one summoned to aid."

Christ is our defender, our upholder. He is always there, at the right hand of God, ready to come to our aid. To plead our case. To intercede on our behalf.

1 John 2:1

My little children, these things write I unto you, that ye sin not. And if any man sin, we have an advocate with the Father, Jesus Christ the righteous.

1 John 1:9 is God's method for maintaining our fellowship with Him. If we sin so that our fellowship is broken, we may renew that fellowship by confessing our sin.

1 John 1:9

⁹If we confess our sins, he is faithful and just to forgive us [our] sins, and to cleanse us from all unrighteousness.

He is unable to act as our advocate unless we confess our sins because Satan has a legal right to torment, oppress and even cause death. The moment we confess them Jesus takes up our case before the Father.

The Word declares that when we confess our sins, He righteous and faithful to forgive us our sins and to cleanse us from all unrighteousness and to wipe them out as though they had never been.

Psalms 103:12

¹²As far as the east is from the west, [so] far hath he removed our transgressions from us.

It is absolutely essential that Christians know Jesus as their advocate. Many who are out of fellowship have confessed their sins many times without receiving a sense of restoration, because they did not know Jesus was their Advocate. They did not take forgiveness when they confessed their sins. They did not act upon the Word, which declared that the Father forgives the moment they confess.

No Christian should ever remain in broken fellowship any longer than it takes to ask forgiveness. What the Father forgives He for gets. A child of His should never dishonor His Word by ever thinking of his sins again.

Remember These Facts

Remission is one of the great words of the New Covenant. It means wiping out as though it had never been. When God remits our sins, they are wiped out as though they had never been. The word **"remission"** is never used but in connection with the New Birth.

After we become Christians, then we have our sins forgiven on the basis of our relationship and the intercession of Christ.

When we come to Him as sinners, and take Christ as Savior, confess Him as our Lord, then all that we have ever done is wiped out.

In the New Birth all that we have ever been, stops being and a New Creation takes the place of the old. Six or eight times the word **"remission"** is translated **"forgiveness"** in the Epistles.

Ephesians 1:7

7In whom we have redemption through his blood, the forgiveness of sins, according to the riches of his grace;

The remission of our sins takes the place of the scapegoat under the First Covenant. It bore away their sins once a year, while the blood covered Israel as a nation. On the basis of the blood of Christ, our sins are remitted and we are re-created. **We can now take Satan to the Supreme Court of Heaven and Win OUR CASE.**

CHAPTER TEN

Blood Is Thicker Than Water

R evelation 12:11
¹¹And they overcame him by the blood of the Lamb, and by the word of their testimony; and they loved not their lives unto the death.

When you got your back against the wall and your big brother or sister shows up the words "**blood is thicker than water**" are the sweetest words that will fall from your lips. All of a certain everything changes we began to have courage, confidence, and fear flee from us. **The Blood of Jesus is secret weapon number one for the Christian that wants to take Satan to court**. If Christians come to an understanding of how precious and powerful the blood of our Savior is in our walk, they would surely cry out loud, "**Blood is thicker than water.**" they would be well on the way to being overcomers. The precious blood of our Lord not only serves as an atonement for our sins but it totally wipes it out and it totally devastates the demonic realm.

1 Peter 1:18-19

¹⁸Forasmuch as ye know that ye were not redeemed with corruptible things, [as] silver and gold, from your vain conversation [received] by tradition from your fathers;

¹⁹But with the precious blood of Christ, as of a lamb without blemish and without spot:

At the mention of the blood of Jesus, demons literally tremble with fear. They may remain silent for a few moments, but they will soon cry out, "**Stop it!**" The blood cleanses in the spirit, and burns the demons. The powers of darkness can never stand against the blood of Jesus Christ.

Like most things in the spirit, faith must be an active ingredient in claiming the blood or using it as a weapon. Faith comes through hearing, and hearing by the Word of God.

The blood is precious to man because it is precious to Righteous Judge. God shows us very early in the Word the importance of blood to Him and all mankind and therefore blood is thicker than water.

Genesis 3:21

²¹Unto Adam also and to his wife did the LORD God make coats of skins, and clothed them.

To obtain skins, blood had to be shed. Adam and Eve covered themselves with fig leaves, but fig leaves will never do. Only blood can provide a covering for mankind. The word "**atonement" means** "covering." Only blood will cover our sins. God already had plans to save mankind. He knew the precious blood of his Son would one day be shed for the world.

In Genesis chapter four, God respected Abel's sacrifice of a lamb, but He rejected Cain's sacrifice of fruits and vegetables. God showed that a sacrifice through blood was the only sacrifice acceptable to Him. Cain misunderstood, and many Christian also misunderstand the importance of the blood. Fig-leaf coverings and vegetable sacrifices will never do. Churches that do not know the power of the blood of Jesus have fig leaf and vegetable ministries.

Cain doubtlessly worked hard for his fruits and vegetables; but no matter how hard he worked, no matter how hard many fruits and vegetables he grew and gathered, it could not provide a covering for sin. In church terms, no matter how many good works a person does, if the Lamb's blood is not in his life, there is no salvation, no atonement, and no pleasing God.

We Need The Word and The Blood

In getting what we legally deserve and taking Satan to court we must learn how to use our spiritual weapons against him. The army of the Lord is powerless until it uses its weapons; these weapons are mighty to the bringing down of strongholds (II Cor. 10:4). They are the Sword of the Spirit, which is the Word of God, and the Blood, for we read in **Rev. 12:11**, "They overcame Satan by the blood of the Lamb and by the word of their testimony." **We need the WORD and the BLOOD.**

If every Christian who names the name of Jesus would plead His **precious Blood every day—out loud**—I believe the result would be catastrophic in Satan's kingdom, and great deliverance would be felt in the Church and in the nation.

So it is clear that no deliverance can be maintained without keeping under the Blood. But as long as we stay under the Blood by faith and obedience, Satan cannot penetrate the Bloodline. We can take him to the Supreme Court and **"WIN."**

In Israel nothing could be obtained from God except on the ground of blood sacrifice. Nor can anything be obtained today except on the ground of the Blood of Jesus, which flows as a healing stream for the spirit, soul and body of man. **We can only come with the PRECIOUS BLOOD OF JESUS to the Righteous Judge,** "*Having therefore, brethren, boldness to enter into the holiest by the blood of Jesus…let us draw near with a true heart in full assurance of faith, having our hearts sprinkled…*" **(Hebrews 10:19-22).**

The Blood, Word, and Spirit Agree

Pleading the blood brings the Holy Spirit like nothing else. You see, the Spirit, water, and blood agree on earth. Water often stands for the Word of God. Ephesians 5:26 says:

Ephesians 5:26

²⁶That he might sanctify and cleanse it with the washing of water by the word,

Blood sanctifies the Word:
Hebrews 9:19

¹⁹For when Moses had spoken every precept to all the people according to the law, he took the blood of calves and of goats, with water, and scarlet wool, and hyssop, and sprinkled both the book, and all the people.

Without the Cross and the blood, the Word alone would not bring salvation. In the Bible "**Word**" in is represented by "**Water.**" So here again, we see that Blood is thicker than water. The Word, therefore, agrees with the blood. The Holy Spirit agrees with the blood. He comes quickly when you claim the blood of Jesus with faith. **1 John 5:8** says,

1 John 5:8

⁸And there are three that bear witness in earth, the Spirit, and the water, and the blood: and these three agree in one.

Mention the blood or the Word, and the Holy Spirit agrees and run to help you defeat Satan, and demons. Plead the blood or confess the Word, and the Spirit responds. God not only inhabits the praises of His people, He responds to the blood and the Word. The Word and the blood agree because it is the blood that empowers the Word and the Word that confesses the blood.

It Washes Clean

In Moses' day, God had His priests put on white linen garments (Lev. 6:10). God was showing mankind heavenly things. Before Jesus walked the earth in flesh. God had to give those who appeared in His heavenly presence holy garments (Zach. 3:5). Isaiah 61:10 says,

Isaiah 61:10

¹⁰ I will greatly rejoice in the LORD, my soul shall be joyful in my God; for he hath clothed me with the garments of salvation, he hath covered me with the robe of righteousness, as a bridegroom decketh [himself] with ornaments, and as a bride adorneth [herself] with her jewels.

After Jesus Christ shed His precious blood for the world, the garments of righteousness could be obtained only through a washing by His blood. Animal sacrifice was no longer acceptable to God. In Revelation 6:11, the Scriptures talk about the martyrs in heaven:

Revelation 6:11

¹¹And white robes were given unto every one of them

Revelation 7:9

⁹After this I beheld, and, lo, a great multitude, which no man could number, of all nations, and kindreds, and people, and tongues, stood before the throne, and before the Lamb, clothed with white robes, and palms in their hands.

Who these saints are and how their robes became white is explained in **Revelation 7:14**:

Revelation 7:14

¹⁴And I said unto him, Sir, thou knowest. And he said to me, These are they which came out of great tribulation, and have washed their robes, and made them white in the blood of the Lamb.

There can be no garments of righteousness without washing by His precious Blood. Jesus said,

Revelation 3:18

¹⁸I counsel thee to buy of me gold tried in the fire, that thou mayest be rich; and white raiment, that thou mayest be clothed, and [that] the shame of thy nakedness do not appear; and anoint thine eyes with eyesalve, that thou mayest see.

His blood covers our sins. When God looks upon us, He does not see our sins. He sees only white garments cleansed by the blood of Jesus and therefore God will hear our case.

The Blood Consecrates

The priests in Moses' day were ordained by placing blood that cleansed them of sin and set them apart for service unto God. God designated the tribe of Levi for priestly duties. Not all Levites were priests, but all priests were Levites. The blood consecrated those called to service in the temple. Jesus Christ, the Son of God, sits at the right hand of the Father. He consecrates Himself for service unto the Father and all of mankind. It is His blood that consecrates and sets aside those who desire to serve through the blood.

The Blood Heals

In the Old Testament, the prescribed way to cleanse a leper was to place the blood of a lamb on his right ear, thumb, and big toe. The blood cleansed the people of all types of diseases. To those in the flesh, it had to be one of the strangest ways to heal sickness, but to God it was the only way. It was a type and shadow for those of us today who believe in Jesus Christ.

It is the blood that heals, and it continues to do so today. It comes from the Son who sits at the right hand of the Father. The Bible promises that we are healed by His stripes **(Isa. 53:51; 1 Pet. 2:24).** Thirty-nine stripes slashed His back, and the cruel whip with a piece of bone at the end tore His flesh and ripped it apart. Under Roman law, a man could not be whipped more than forty times, and if the person administering the whipping exceeded that amount, he would in turn be punished severely. Therefore, to make sure that forty stripes was not exceeded accidentally, they stopped at thirty-nine.

Medical books separate all types of disease and sickness into thirty-nine categories. It is no coincidence that a number of stripes on His back was thirty-nine. It's the blood from the stripes that heals. Jesus sits in glory at the right hand of the Father, but His blood still heals on earth. Its power can never be lost.

The Blood Saves

God took careful steps to teach us about the saving power of the blood. Rahab, the harlot who along with her family was saved from destruction, was instructed to tie a scarlet thread on her window. When Jericho's walls fell, only Rahab's house was spared. No lamb available, so the spies used a scarlet thread. That scarlet thread represented blood. It saved Rahab and her entire family.

It was the crucifixion of Jesus Christ the Son of God that tore the veil between God and man and brought reconciliation **(Rom. 5:10; 2 Cor. 5:18)**. Now, we call Him Abba Father, and He calls us sons and daughters. The blood made it possible for the prodigal sons to come home. It saves!

The Blood Atones

It is the blood that atones for the soul.

Leviticus 17:11

¹¹For the life of the flesh [is] in the blood: and I have given it to you upon the altar to make an atonement for your souls: for it [is] the blood [that] maketh an atonement for the soul.

That is why God so strongly admonished the people against eating or drinking blood. Blood is precious. One cannot disrespect it or look upon it in a trivial manner. God will not allow it because one day, His beloved Son would shed His blood for mankind and wash away the veil between the Father and us.

The blood atones or covers sin. **Hebrews 9:22** says:

Hebrews 9:22

²²And almost all things are by the law purged with blood; and withoutshedding of blood is no remission.

Without His blood, we would be forever doomed.

The Blood Turns Away Death

When Moses led the people of God out of Egypt, God again demonstrated the power of the blood. God showed us that the blood turns away even death. In **Exodus 12:7 and 13**. God instructed Moses to have the people kill a perfect lamb, one for each household of fifteen people, and to sprinkle its blood on the side posts and lintel of the door. When the Angel of Death passed by, it did not enter any household with the blood so sprinkled, for God did not allow it to enter. Death is an enemy. The Bible says that Jesus will sit at the right hand of the Father until all of His enemies are put under his feet.

1 Corinthians 15:25

^{25}For he must reign, till he hath put all enemies under his feet.

^{26}The last enemy [that] shall be destroyed [is] death.

Life defeats death. The Bible says that the life is in the blood—not the heart, kidneys, or brains **(Lev. 17:11, 14)**. The life of Jesus is in His blood. It is the life in the blood that turns back death.

Only God's perfect Passover Lamb, Jesus Christ, will do. It is His blood that protects us from death and gives us everlasting life. His blood compels death to pass over. No fig leaves or fruits will do it, no good works just faith, the grace of God, and the blood of the Lamb.

CHAPTER ELEVEN

It's Who You Know That Counts

The second most powerful weapon that we need to have and know how to use is **"The Name of Jesus."** Jesus has **"given the Body of Christ the Power of Attorney to use His Name"** against Satan and his army and anything that we want. We all know the importance of knowing someone that is very important, they can help you get a job, credit, or if you know the son of the judge in court you can have an edge that others may not have.

Likewise if you know the Son of the Highest Judge in Heaven and on Earth even under the Earth and You know His Son, this will make all the difference you need. Knowing Him will sure make a difference when taking Satan to court. **"Truly it is who you know that counts."** All men have the legal and redemptive right to use the name of Jesus in asking and receiving from God. **This puts prayer on a purely legal basis.**

We are entering into the era of dominion linked with Omnipotence, filled with Him who is is greater than he that is in the world, with the wisdom of Him who spoke a universe into being, and with a legal right to use His Name in every crisis of our lives.

John 14:13-14 "*¹³And whatsoever ye shall ask in my name, that will I do, that the Father may be glorified in the Son. ¹⁴If ye shall ask any thing in my name, I will do it.*"

This is not prayer. The promise of the use of His Name in prayer is given in the 15th and 16th chapters.

It is what Peter used at the beautiful gate of the temple as recorded in **Acts 3**. He used the Name. He said, "***In the Name of Jesus Christ of Nazareth, walk.***" That man who had been lame from birth leaped to his feet, perfectly well and strong. Jesus said, "Whatsoever ye shall demand in my Name **(for the word ask means demand) I will do it.**" "In my Name they shall cast out demons." In His Name you can take Satan to court and win. There is no prayer about that, that is where we come to this bound and afflicted man or woman and say, "**In the Name of Jesus, Satan we charge you to leave this body, take every demon with you and go back to Hell where you belong!**"

Satan knows he is defeated, and when we use the Name he must leave. **John 15:16** "*That whatsoever ye shall ask of the Father in my Name, He may give it you.*" **This is prayer.**

You remember the word "ask" in the Greek means "demand."

You are not demanding it of God. You are demanding that forces that are injurious shall be broken, that diseases shall be healed, that circumstances shall be changed, that money shall come that Satan has stolen.

Jesus is going to look after this thing that you demand in His Name.

Read carefully John 16:24-27 and you will catch a glimpse of your legal right to use the Name of Jesus. "***Hitherto you have asked nothing in my name. Ask and ye shall receive that your joy may be made full.***"

You have noticed the absence of the word "**believe**" or the word "**faith**." In all three of these wonderful chapters with these great promises, the words "**faith**" or "**believe**" do not occur. **WHY!!!!** Because we are in the family, and because we are in the family we have a legal right to these things. **Eph. 1:3** illustrates it, "*³Blessed be the God and Father of our Lord Jesus Christ, who hath blessed is with every spiritual blessing in the heavenly places in Christ.*" What Jesus did was for us.

The Name Of Jesus does Not Work Without The Blood

There are some who tell us that it is enough that we have the name of Jesus. But not so. We need the Name of Jesus and the Blood, for the life is in the Blood. There is power in the name of Jesus only because He shed His Own Blood and offered it to His Father, Who thereupon gave His power and His authority to His Son **(Matthew 28:18)**. That same power and authority is given to all believers **(Luke 10:19)**, but it only becomes operative as we honor His Blood.

The Name of Jesus Means Much To The Father

The protection afforded us by the Blood rests in the fact that Jesus' Blood says something to God. The Blood cries out to God, "**Sin is covered and forgiven and remitted! The penalty is paid!**"

The name of Jesus means much to the Father. He will always honor this name because of the following reasons:

It means to Him that redemption has been completed and the world is saved from eternal rule by satanic powers.

It means to the Father that His eternal plan of a perfect and sinless society on Earth and in the whole universe is guaranteed. This means more to the Father than our finite minds can now grasp because of the lack of understanding of the scope of the plan of God for man.

The Father recognizes all that the name of Jesus implies. He knows that we have a legal and family right to use this name in prayer.

The Father knows that the right use of this name will deliver all men from sin, sickness, and failure in life.

It is the glory of God to recognize the name of Jesus in prayer and to answer according to the faith exercised.

The Name of Jesus Means Much To Satan

To Satan and demons, the name of Jesus means their utter defeat, humiliation, banishment to the lowest Hell. It means they are now defeated and that they have to loose any person that they control in any degree when the name of Jesus is used against them. They obey that name and fear and tremble when it is used in faith. They flee when they are resisted and rebuked by this name.

The Name of Jesus Means Much To The Church

To the church, the name of Jesus means that **ANY THING** that is needed or wanted in life now and hereafter will be granted when it is used in unwavering faith. All the infinite resources of God belong to the church, and nothing is impossible to the believer who launches out into full and free use of the name of Jesus.

God's plan for the church is to get and use the full power of attorney and carry on business for God and Christ by the power of the Holy Spirit as Christ carried on the work of God by the Spirit when He was on Earth.

If there is any failure to carry on this work, and do even greater works than Christ did, it is not because redemption is not complete and man's case has been lost in the Highest Court of Heaven. It is not because the devil is stronger than God. It is not because the Holy Spirit has failed enduing men with power. It is simply because the church has failed as a whole and individuals have failed in particular to exercise their God given rights and privileges as taught in the gospel, and become endued with power from on high.

HOW TO USE THE NAME

This is the most vital truth to every one of us. How I have studied this problem. The Name of Jesus is used in two major ways. First, in prayer to the Father. **John 15:16** "*16And whatsoever ye shall ask of the Father in my name He may give it to you.*"

John 16:23, "*²³If ye shall ask anything of the Father in my name He will give it to you.*" Prayer is to be made to the Father, in Jesus' Name, not to the Holy Spirit or Jesus. This is Divine order. Your judgment or my judgment or any other man's opinion is of no value.

"**When you pray, say our Father.**" Jesus stands between the Father and us in His mediatorial, High Priestly ministry to make it good.

He declares that whatsoever we ask in that Name the Father will give it to us. That is final. That is absolute. **John 14:13-34** He tells us how to use the Name of Jesus in sickness or in adverse circumstances, or any other crisis.

This is the way I use the Name: Here is a case of **"Cancer."** I lay my hands on him and say, "**In the Name of Jesus Christ, body obey the Word. The Word declares that "by His stripes you are healed**," I command you, spirit of Cancer to leave this body now."

The demon of sickness leaves, and the person is healed.

Biblical Proof for the Christian's Power of Attorney

"*Where two or three are gathered IN MY NAME, there am I in the midst of them*" **(Matt. 18:19-20).**

"*These signs shall follow them that believe; IN MY NAME shall they cast out devils; they shall speak with new tongues; they shall take up serpents and if they drink any deadly thing it shall not hurt them; they shall lay hands on the sick, and they shall recover*" **(Mark 16:15-20).**

It's Who You Know That Counts

"*Verily, verily, I say unto you, He that believeth on me, the works that I do shall he do also; and greater works than these shall he do; because I go unto my Father. And WHATSOEVER ye shall ask IN MY NAME, that will I do, that the Father may be glorified in the Son. If you shall ask any thing IN MY NAME, I will do it*" **(John 14:12-15).**

"*Ye have not chosen me, but I have chosen you, and ordained you, that ye should go and bring forth fruit, and that your fruit should remain: that WHATSOEVER ye shall ask the Father IN MY NAME, he may give it you*"**(John 15:16).**

"WHATSOEVER ye shall ask the Father IN MY NAME, he will give it you. Hitherto have ye ask nothing IN MY NAME: ask and ye shall receive, that your joy may be full...At that day ye shall ask IN MY NAME," **(John 16:23-26).**

These statements are the direct words of Jesus Himself and certainly express the Christian's power of attorney. He has given us unqualified use of His name to carry on the work of God in this world. All that God has invested in **His Name** is **Ours**.

As Paul expressed it, *"All things are yours...And ye are Christ's; and Christ's is God's"* **(1 Cor. 3:21-23).** He gives us assurance that all prayer prayed **IN HIS NAME** will receive the special attention of both Himself and His Father and our Father. It is just like saying, **"You ask of the Father IN MY NAME; I will endorse it, and the Father will give it."**

If modern Christians could only wake up and realize their rights in the New Testament, and would exercise their full authority according to their rights, there would be no failure, no sin, no bad habits, no unhappiness, no defeat no sickness, and no want among them. All of our wants have been promised by God, not only our needs.

When men pray in the name of Jesus they pray by **HIS AUTHORITY**, and it is as if Jesus Himself were praying.

The Churches Problem

The church as a whole today does not understand the true purpose of the body of Christ in the world. The average minister does not understand the true issues between God and Satan. Satan is taking advantage of this ignorance and unbelief and holding back the great usefulness of the church in the Earth. He is defeating Christians by the millions. He is making them believe that it is not God's will for them to get what they want in this life. He makes them fear to use the name of Jesus in prayer and in daily conflicts against him and his demon forces. As long as the church lives in this ignorance it will be defeated in doing the works of God that should be manifest today in every local church as it was in the early churches.

The Purpose of The Power of Attorney

The purpose of the power of attorney and its normal use among men is to confirm the Word of God and prove to men that God is the Supreme Being of the universe. All representatives of God should be like Paul, who said to the Romans, "I will not dare to speak of any of those things which Christ hath not wrought by me, to make the Gentiles obedient BY WORD AND DEED, through mighty signs and wonders, by the power of the Spirit of God.... I have fully preached the gospel of Christ...And I am sure that, when I come unto you, I shall come in the fulness of the blessing of the gospel of Christ" **(Rom. 15:18-19, 29)**. He said to the Corinthians, "I will come unto you shortly, if the Lord will, and will know, not the speech of them which are puffed up, but the power. **FOR THE KINGDOM OF GOD IS NOT IN WORD, BUT IN POWER**" **(1 Cor. 4:18-20)**.

CHAPTER TWELVE

We Know Someone Who Judges Ear

Do you know anyone that when you are talking they are, so to speak, **"All Ears?"** When Jesus Christ talks to the Father, the High Supreme Court Judge, He is all Ears. God always hears Jesus, as proved in the gospel records. At the grave of Lazarus He said, "Father, I thank thee that thou hast heard me. **And I knew that thou headrest me ALWAYS" (John 11:41-42).** If Christians would pray by **HIS AUTHORITY** and realize the power of such prayer, they would have more confidence in answered prayer. They would realize that God always hears Jesus, and that when they pray by His authority it will always be answered. When you are connected to Jesus you are connected to the Father. In **1 John 2:23** it says, *"Whosoever denieth the Son, the same hath not the Father: [(but) he that acknowledgeth the Son hath the Father also]."* You can't loose when you know Jesus and He knows you.

When men pray in the name of Jesus they should not only believe that they are praying by His authority but also that the prayers pass into His hands, and that He assumes responsibility for the answer. He says, *"**WHATSOEVER** ye shall ask **IN MY NAME, THAT WILL I DO**"* and *"**I WILL DO IT**"* (**John 14:12-15**). He said of the Father, *"**WHATSOEVER** ye shall ask **IN MY NAME, HE WILL GIVE IT YOU**"* (**John 16:23-26**).

Paul said of the Father, *"He that spared not His own Son, but delivered him up for **US ALL**, how shall he not with him **ALSO FREELY GIVE US ALL THINGS**"* (Rom. 8:32).

Jesus Takes Our Case Before The Father

Christ is not only our **SUBSTITUTE** in atonement, but He also takes our place before God to ever live and make intercession for us according to the will of God (**Rom. 8:34; Heb. 7:25**). His work then was not completed at the cross. He still is our **HIGH PRIEST** before God (**Heb. 4:14-16**). He is our **ADVOCATE or DEFENCE ATTORNEY** when we are accused before God by the Satan or the devil (**1 John 2:1-2; Rev. 12:10**).

Where is there any room for failure to get what is asked if we would only come boldly to the throne of grace to obtain mercy to help in time of need and leave our case in His hands, as we are commanded to do in (**Heb. 4:14-16; 10:19-23**). There can be no failure in any one case if true and unwavering faith is exercised (**James 1:5-8; Heb. 11:6**). Prayer is a business proposition and should be the chief business of our lives. This is true because the chief business of our lives needs much prayer to make it a success.

The Bible is A Legal Document

The Holy Bible is a legal document which will Stand up in the Court of Heaven for you are against you. The Bible says in **2 Peter 1:21**, *"²¹For the prophecy came not in old time by the will of man: but holy men of God spake [as they were] moved by the Holy Ghost."* It also says in **Romans 2:16**, *"¹⁶In the day when God shall judge the secrets of men by Jesus Christ according to my gospel."* The Bible that you hold in your hand and hardly ever read will be your judge. God reminds us in **2 Timothy 2:15**, *"¹⁵Study to shew thyself approved unto God, a workman that needeth not to be ashamed, rightly dividing the word of truth."* Also in **Matthew 22:29** we read, *"²⁹Jesus answered and said* *unto them, Ye do err, not knowing the scriptures, nor the power of God."* Further the Word say, in Hosea 4:6 it says, *"**My people are destroyed for lack of knowledge.**"* Our success in taking Satan to court will correspond directly to the amount of time we spend in the Word of God.

The Last Commission of Jesus

The above Scriptures about praying IN HIS NAME were the last words that Christ uttered before He ascended to the Father. They are part of the commission of the church in evangelizing the world and reconciling it to God. In these passages we have the Christians power of attorney covering the defeat of satanic forces that hinder the gospel work. *"**IN MY NAME they shall cast out devils.**"* This was true of the first preaching tours of the disciples before the cross **(Matt. 10:1-20; Luke 9:1-9; 10:1-20; Mark 6:7-13)**; and this was true after the cross **(Acts 2:43; 3:6-7; 5:12-16; 6:8; 8:1-21; 16:16-34; 19:11-20)**.

There is power in the name of Jesus. The demons said, *"**Jesus I know, and Paul I know,**"* that is, we know that Jesus and Paul were our masters and we obey them, but we know nothing about you seven men whom we have never met in combat **(Acts 19:11-20)**. Jesus said, *"**ALL AUTHORITY is given unto me in heaven and in earth**"* **(Matt. 28:18)**.

By HIS AUTHORITY men was commissioned to go into all the world and preach the gospel to every creature, and God would stand by them and defeat all demons powers IN THE NAME OF JESUS. This was to continue *"**even unto the end of the world**"* **(Matt. 28:18-20)**.

In other words, if men will go and preach the truth, it will set men free from demon power wherever and as long as truth is preached. Jesus sent the disciples in all nations and promised to back them up with signs following which would confirm the preached word **(Mark 16:15-20; Heb. 2:3-4)**.

All men who preach have a perfect right to cast out devils and to have all the signs of the gospel following them. If this is not true of them, they are poor representations of God and are failing to do as God commissions them.

How Did Jesus Get This Power To Give To Me?

There are several ways in which Christ obtained all authority in Heaven and in Earth to give to men to carry on His work throughout this age. If men are to be given the power of attorney it should be clear to them that Christ has the right to give them that power and the extent to which it is to be by them. *The following is the sevenfold way Christ obtained His great name and the power of attorney:*

HIS DEITY. By virtue of being God by nature, and of being the creative agent in the making and upholding of all things. He has the right to have this authority. As God He could be the only one capable of this honor **(Col. 1:15-18; Heb. 1:1-3).**

BY BIRTH. Not only because of His deity, but also because of His humanity. Christ has obtained this place before God and man as the Saviour, Life-giver, and the Power of God. *"Thou shalt call his name JESUS: for he shall save his people from their sins"* **(Matt. 1:21).**

This person was **Immanuel** or God with us **(Matt. 1:23; Isa. 7:14; 9:6-7).** Jesus was born to be the King of the Jews and the Saviour of the world **(John 19:36-37; Luke 2:11, 25-32).**

BY HIS SINLESSNESS. Jesus was the only human being that ever lived without sin since the fall. He was the only one that could atone for man, for the substitute had to be sinless. He was made in the likeness of flesh that sin controlled, but His flesh was not sinful flesh or under the dominion of sin, as was that of all other men **(Rom. 8:1-3; 2 Cor. 5:21; 1 Pet. 2:21-25).** Because of His sinless life God blessed Him above all other men: *"Thou hast loved righteousness, and hated iniquity; therefore, God, even thy God, hath anointed thee with the oil of gladness above thy fellows"* **(Heb. 2:9).**

BY HIS PREPARATION. From childhood Christ prepared Himself for the work that His Father sent Him into the world to do.

BY HIS ANOINTING. Because of His humanity and earthly limitations as a man and because of His sinlessness and preparation for a divine anointing, God gave Him the full anointing of the Holy Spirit to enable Him to achieve greatness in three worlds—Heaven, Earth, and Hell. By this anointing, as predicted in **Isa. 11:1-2; 43:1-7; 61:1-2**; and fulfilled in **Matt. 3:16-17; Luke 4:16-21; Acts 10:38; John 3:34**, He gained eternal fame in all the universe.

BY HIS ACHIEVEMENTS. By what He accomplished for God and man He is great. Death, Hell, and the grave were mastered by Him, as well as sin and demons on Earth. Every enemy of both God and man was fully conquered. Redemption was made complete. God and man became reconciled, and God's eternal plan for man will be realized. His fame even reached to the highest Heaven and the lowest Hell, and all creatures must bow the knees to Him **(Phil. 2:5-11; Col. 1:16-21; 2:14-17; Eph. 1:20-23; Heb. 2:14-15; 1 Pet. 3:22; Rev. 5:1-14; 12:11).** His achievements in life on Earth are recorded in the gospels as being so many that if they were written, even the world could not contain

the books that should be written **(John 21:25)**. His achievements in death were even greater than those in life. For His work in death, God has highly exalted Him above every name, and every tongue must confess Him as Lord to the glory of God the Father **(Phil. 2:5-11)**.

BY INHERITANCE. Paul speaks of Christ as having been appointed "heir of all things...he hath by inheritance obtained a more excellent name than they" (the angels, Heb. 1:1-14). Some men have obtained a great name and fame by birth, by being great students, by making thorough preparation for some specific work, and by their achievements; but no other man has obtained such fame in all realms of the universe as Christ and by al the means by which He became famous. Some men have obtained temporary and local fame, but Christ, by all the above mentioned means, has gained universal and eternal fame.

It is this **SUPER-EXALTED-ETERNAL** person that has **AUTHORITY** in Heaven and in Earth and who wants to confer the **POWER OF ATTORNEY** upon all believers. He will represent you before the Court of Heaven.

All Believers Are Encouraged to Do What Jesus Did

Now all believers can do the works of Christ and greater works than what He did, because, as He said, "I go unto my Father" **(John 14:12-15)**.

He is today exalted at the right of the majesty on high, angels, principalities, and powers being made subject unto Him **(Eph. 1:20-23; 1 Pet. 3:22)**.

He now upholds all things by the word of His power, and, as the Head of the Church and as the Custodian of the power of attorney, He can and does bestow full and legal authority upon all believers who get to know the truth and who will tarry until they are fully endued with power from on high **(Luke 24:49; Acts 1:8)**.

CHAPTER THIRTEEN

I Have A Right To Use My Savior Name

Everything that Jesus did He did it for me. Therefore I have a right to use His Name to Take Satan to Court. All Christians are commanded to use the name of Jesus in salvation **(Matt. 1:21; Acts 4:12)** ; in baptism **(Matt. 28:19)**; in healing **(Acts 3:6-7, 16)**; in preaching **(Luke 24:47; Acts 8:12)**; in miracles **(Acts 3:16; 4:30; Mark 9:29)**; in judgment **(1 Cor. 5:1-5)**; in appeals to others **(1 Cor. 1:10)**; in prayer **(John 14:12-15; 16:23-26)**; in faith and repentance **(John 1:12; 3:18; Acts 10:43)**; in praise **(Heb. 13:15)**; in all gatherings **(Matt. 18:20)**; in consecration **(Matt. 19:29)**; in charity **(Mark 9:41)**; in singing **(Rom. 15:9)**; in combat **(Mark 16:17; Luke 10-17; Eph. 6:10-18)**; and in all things **(Col. 3:17; Eph. 5:20)**.

Disciples Before The Cross Used His Name

The disciples before the cross used His name to defeat Satan **(Matt. 10:1-20; Mark 6:7-13; Luke 9:1-6; 10:1-20)**. The Word says in **Romans 8:37**, "³⁷*Nay, in all these things we are more than* *conquerors through him that loved us."* Even men who did not follow the apostolic band did miracle in the name of Jesus (**Luke 9:48-50**). These disciples were commanded to use His name to get whatever they wanted (**John 14:12-15; 15:16; 16:23-26**). They used His name.

Disciples After The Cross Used His Name

Disciples after the cross used His name and turned the world upside down (**Acts 2:38-39; 3:6-16; 4:5-18, 29-30; 5:12-16, 28, 41; 8:12; 9:15-17, 27-29; 16:16-18; 19:11-20; 26:9**).

Not only do the gospels and the book of Acts teach the Christian's use of the power of attorney, but in all the epistles we have scores of references as to how believers are to use the name of Jesus in every phase of life (**1 Cor. 1:2, 10; 5:4; 6:11; Eph. 5:20; Phil. 2:5-11; Col. 3:17; 2 Thess. 1:11-12; 3:6; Heb. 13:15; James 2:7; 5:14; 1 Pet. 4:14; 1 John 2:12; 3:23; 5:13**). In **2 Thess. 1:11-12** we have a prayer that the name of Jesus should be glorified in saints. How can we glorify His name other than in the way the early church did? The name of Jesus was preached among the heathen, and it wrought such miraculous things that multitudes turned to God. They represented His name and used it to defeat all demon powers. This name became the center of all work for God. This should be the place His name holds in all modern church work. When this becomes true again men will have and use the Christian's power of attorney.

The Reason I have The Right To Use My Savior Name

IT IS OUR GOSPEL RIGHT. The gospel is still the power of God unto salvation to everyone that believes (**Rom. 1:16**). The word "salvation here means full deliverance by the power of God from sin, sickness, failure, powerlessness, and known needs of the human life.

IT IS OUR REDEMPTIVE RIGHT. Redemption means that God has bought us and that we belong to Him and we are not our own (**1 Cor. 6:19-20**).

IT IS OUR NEEDFUL RIGHT. From the standpoint of need as children of God we have a right to claim as full a supply as God has promised **(Phil. 4:19).**

IT IS OUR PROMISE RIGHT. All the promises of God are for all who believe, but not one thing is promised the unbeliever **(2 Cor. 1:20; 2 Pet. 1:3-4).**

IT IS OUR FAMILY RIGHT. As sons of God men naturally have power by virtue of the relationship with God **(John 1:12; 2 Tim. 1:7).**

IT IS OUR LEGAL RIGHT. Legal rights to use the name of Christ is promised every believer.

IT IS OUR COMMISSIONED RIGHT. Every child of God has been commissioned to use the name of Jesus **(Matt. 29:18-20; John 14:12-15; 15:16; 16:23-26).**

CHAPTER FOURTEEN

Our Soul Are Woven Together In AGAPE Love

Agape, Greek agapē, in the New Testament, the fatherly love of God for humans, as well as the human reciprocal love for God. In Scripture, the transcendent agape love is the highest form of love and is contrasted with eros, or erotic love, and philia, or brotherly love.

The Lord's table is a confession of our faith and our loyalty to love, just as the Father's giving Jesus is a confession of His love. Jesus' coming and giving Himself for us was a confession of His love.

They were both loyal to love. Jesus said these significant words in **1 Corinthians 11:26**, "*²⁶For as often as ye eat this bread, and drink this cup, ye do shew the Lord's death till he come.*" It was a "Covenant." He said, "This is my blood of the New Covenant." As often as you drink the cup, you ratify this Covenant. It is a love Covenant.

The word "**ratify**" means to accept and sanction formally, confirm; establish. First, it is your loyalty and love to Jesus. Second, it is your loyalty and love for His Body, the Church. It is a confession of your love one for another. It is a confession that you have eaten and drunk with them, and now you are going to bear their burdens. When we partake of the Holy Communion with a brother or sister our souls are woven together in love.

You have identified yourself with each other, just as He identified Himself with you in His Incarnation and Substitution. That would be the Master's attitude toward the Lord's table.

When I break the bread and drink the cup, I not only confess my loyalty to Him, but to every member of the Body of Christ who breaks that bread and drinks that cup with me. If I am strong, I bear the burdens of the weak. I have taken over their weaknesses.

The Holy Communion means that I will never criticize, but I will assume their spiritual responsibilities and weaknesses. Someone is going to rise and understand this. Some body of people is going to enter into it.

The Curse On The Body Of Christ

It has been said that the eleven o'clock hour is the most segregated hour in the Body of Chris. This is when most Christian are worshipping God through Jesus Christ and taking Holy Communion. This is when most races come together to worship their God. White with white, black with black and Koreans with Koreans, etc. We act as if each race got its on heaven to go to.

There is but one body and each Christian is a member of that body regardless of race. The Word of God says in **Galatians 3:28**, "*28There is neither Jew nor Greek, there is neither bond nor free, there is neither male nor female: for ye are all one in Christ Jesus.*" Also in **Romans 12:4-5** it says, "*4For as we have many members in one body, and all members have not the same office: 5So we, [being] many, are one body in Christ, and every one members one of another.*" I am sorry to burst your bubble, disrupt you comfort zone or rain on your parade but if you want your on heaven you will have to create it yourself. I personally would like to see you take on that task. There is no

Heaven for one particular race. In **Revelation 7:9-10** it says, *"⁹After this I beheld, and, lo, a great multitude, which no man could number, of all nations, and kindreds, and people, and tongues, stood before the throne, and before the Lamb, clothed with white robes, and palms in their hands; ¹⁰And cried with a loud voice, saying, Salvation to our God which sitteth upon the throne, and unto the Lamb."*

The Lord commands Us To Love One Another

The Lord Jesus, before He ascended into Heaven gave his disciples a new commandment and the visible evidence of being born-again and of keeping this command can be seen by all men and can be determined by the manifestation of love for each other in the Body of Christ. We read this new commandment in **John 13:34-35,** *"³⁴A new commandment I give unto you, That ye love one another; as I have loved you, that ye also love one another. ³⁵By this shall all [men] know that ye are my disciples, if ye have love one to another."* This commandment was given by Jesus because of the conflict between the Jew and the gentiles being converted to Christianity. It is the same problem that we are having in the Body of Christ today.

The command to love was new because Jesus gave it a new standard. Moses said, *"love your neighbor as yourself"* **(see Leviticus 19:18).** Jesus said the new standard was, **as I have loved you**. Jesus gave His disciples the example of love that they were to follow. How have Jesus loved you? He said **"By this"** unbelievers recognize Jesus' disciples not by their denomination, not by their miracles, nor even by their love for the lost. They recognize His disciples by their deeds of love for one another. **Psalms 133:1** says, "Behold, how good and how pleasant [it is] for brethren to dwell together in unity"

How Does The World See Us?

Because of the racial differences and division in the Body of Christ the world sees us as divided and want nothing to do with such confusion. It says in **1 Corinthians 14:33,** *"³³For God is not [the author] of confusion, but of peace, as in all churches of the saints."* If God is not the author of this confusion, then guess who is. Yes, that's right it is Satan himself. It says in **Mark 3:24-26**, "*²⁴And if a kingdom be divided against itself, that kingdom cannot stand. ²⁵And if a house be divided against itself, that house cannot stand. ²⁶And if Satan rise up against himself, and be divided, he cannot stand, but hath an end.*"

Now according to the above scriptures the logical conclusion for the Body of Christ in the Earth is if the Body of Christ is divided against itself it cannot stand. And this is precisely why we cannot be a greater spiritual force in the earth for Jesus Christ because we are still divided.

We Can't Take Satan To Court.

We have not kept this commandment to *"love one another as Christ have loved us,"* and because of this we can't take Satan to court until we confess and forsake this practice and attitude. It says in **Proverbs 28:13**, "*¹³He that covereth his sins shall not prosper: but whoso confesseth and forsaketh [them] shall have mercy.*"

We take Holy Communion in our churches with sin on our conscious, but the Bible is clear about breaking this covenant with the Godhead and the Body of Christ. The Bible says in **1 Corinthians 11:27-32**, "*²⁷Wherefore whosoever shall eat this bread, and drink [this] cup of the Lord, unworthily, shall be guilty of the body and blood of the Lord. ²⁸But let a man examine himself, and so let him eat of [that] bread, and drink of [that] cup. ²⁹For he that eateth and drinketh unworthily, eateth and drinketh damnation to himself, not discerning the Lord's body. ³⁰For this cause many [are] weak and sickly among you, and many sleep. ³¹For if we would judge ourselves, we should not be judged. ³²But when we are judged, we are chastened of the Lord, that we should not be condemned with the world.*"

If you can't keep this commandment you may not be saved and will not have to worry about who is going to be there because you may not be there.

The Eleventh Hour

I believe that this is the eleventh hour message, that this is the message for the Church today. In the troubled days that lie ahead, we are going to require all that God can give us, and be to us, to stand the tests we are going through and will go through. The book of Revelation reveals to us the consummation of Satan plans designs, and schemes for the Earth.

You see, brethren, this blood covenant teaching, this relationship teaching, this ability to use the blood of Jesus and the Name of Jesus, this marvelous teaching of our identification and the ministry of Jesus in Heaven, our privileges, and our legal right to take Satan to the Supreme Court of Heaven, is the message for the coming days. It will empower us to meet the very forces of darkness.

Do you know that Jesus, in the Great Commission in the Gospel of Mark, did a peculiar thing? He said, *"In My Name ye shall cast out demons."* We have not seen its significance. We know now what it means. In the last days demons are going to become very prominent.

Satan, knowing that his days are shortened, in coming to the earth with all his host, and we are going to pass into a period of spiritual conflict such as the church has never known. This will not only be persecution, but it will be demons breaking and crushing the spirit of the church in the individual.

The church must learn the secret of standing against the hosts of darkness and

TAKE SATAN TO COURT IN THE NAME OF JESUS.
ARE YOU READY FOR THE RAPTURE?

Meaning of Rapture

It's true that the word rapture is not in the Bible. But neither will you find the Trinity by name in the Bible, nor the word mission and a number of other terms we use to describe theological concepts clearly taught in Scripture.

The word "rapture" is taken from the Latin "rapio" for the two words "caught up" used in **1 Thessalonians 4:17**. It has come into popular use today to refer to the Lord Jesus coming for the church, to lift her up into the heavens. One raptured is "lifted up" in love.

THE HOLY SPIRIT IS THE RESTRAINER

That leaves the Holy Spirit Himself and there happens to be Biblical precedent for both His restraining influence and His abrupt withdrawal before a worldwide judgment. In support of His restraining influence, **John 16:8** has the Lord saying the role of the Holy Spirit is to convict the world of guilt in regard to sin, and righteousness, and judgment. Notice the Lord didn't say He would convict only believers, but the world, believers or not. The Greek word John used there is *"kosmos"*, which means the whole world.

EVERYONE INTUITIVELY KNOWS THERE'S A GOD

Just as everyone INTUITIVELY (know automatically) knows there's a God **(Romans 1:18-20),** everyone intuitively knows right from wrong. Paul said even those who don't have the law will do things the law requires by nature because the requirements of the law are written on our hearts, and our consciences will accuse or defend our actions accordingly **(Romans 2:14-15)**. I believe the "guilty conscience" that even unbelievers experience when they do wrong is the Holy Spirit convicting them in regard to sin, righteousness, and judgment. Throughout the Church Age this conviction has been a major restraining force against evil in the world.

WORLDWIDE HAPPENING NOW IN 2021

In **1 Tim. 4:1-2** Paul wrote, *"The Spirit clearly says that in later times some will abandon the faith and follow deceiving spirits and things taught by demons. Such teachings come through hypocritical liars whose consciences have been seared as with a hot iron."* (In Paul's time applying a fire-heated piece of metal to a wound was an accepted way to help stop the bleeding and close the wound. It's called cauterization, an extremely painful process that left a hideous scar.)

This tells us the current trend of making good appear to be evil and vice versa is a sign that the end is near. Hypocritical liars from inside and outside the church have been causing a gigantic paradigm shift in the world. They intuitively know the things they are trying to teach us are wrong and the conviction of the Holy

Spirit has wounded their consciences. By repeatedly suppressing the guilt they feel they've effectively "cauterized" their consciences to close the wound. This has left their consciences hideously scarred, but allows them to continue spreading their lies without feeling the guilt.

In the process they've also destroyed their powers of discernment which means that each succeeding lie is easier to accept and repeat than the one before it. We've seen the proof of this as things our parents' generation would have abhorred are now being celebrated in ours.

As for the Holy Spirit being temporarily taken out of the way, **Genesis 6:1-3** tells of the time before the Great Flood when certain angels rebelled against God, exchanged their angelic form for human form and began having children with human women. **Genesis 6:4** calls these children the Nephilim. They apparently had incredible skills and abilities and eventually led the whole world astray. Before long the entire creation had been irreparably corrupted.

"³Then the Lord said, My Spirit will not contend with humans forever, for they are mortal; their days will be a hundred and twenty years" **(Genesis 6:3)**

NOAH AND HIS FAMILY ARE NOT CORRUPTED

Noah and his family had not been genetically corrupted by this hybrid invasion. The Lord commissioned him and his sons to build an ark to preserve themselves, their wives, and selected animals and 120 years after His pronouncement He destroyed the whole world in the Great Flood.

The Hebrew word translated "contend" in **Genesis 6:3** means *"to act as a judge"*. In other words the role of the Holy Spirit in pre-flood times was to convict the world of guilt in regard to sin, and righteousness, and judgment just like He's doing in our time **(John 16:8)**. And before the flood God said there would come a time when His Spirit would step aside and allow a time of judgment to proceed, just like Paul said the restrainer would do at the end of the age.

So The Holy Spirit has been holding back the secret power of lawlessness and will continue to do so until He is taken out of the way. All things considered, I believe the Bible makes a compelling case in support of the Holy Spirit being the restrainer Paul spoke of in 2nd Thessalonians. You can almost hear the footsteps of the Messiah.

CHAPTER FIFTEEN

Is Our Relationship With Jesus Real?

Matthew 7:22-23

²²Many will say to me in that day, Lord, Lord, have we not prophesied in thy name? and in thy name have cast out devils? and in thy name done many wonderful works?

²³And then will I profess unto them, I never knew you: depart from me, ye that work iniquity.

The saddest most painful sound coming from Jesus when you try to take Satan to court is *"I never knew you: depart from me you that work iniquity"* or you that played church. The reason that Jesus never knew you is because you never knew Him. You had no intimate relationship with Him.

We have never been identified with Him. Do you know Him well enough to put you case in His hand. You must have a relationship. To have a relationship is more than going to church on Sunday morning, singing in the choir, and looking at your watch to see how much time you got left . It means more than teaching a half or none prepared watered down Sunday school lesson or Bible study. It means more than every once in a while we send up a lukewarm prayer with no power.

Yes we can have the gift of prophecy and bring glory to His Name and you can cast out devils? And you can do many wonderful works and when you stand before Jesus looking for your reward, your mansion in the Heaven instead of hearing the words in **Matthew 25:21**, *"²¹His lord said unto him, Well done, [thou] good and faithful servant: thou hast been faithful over a few things, I will make thee ruler over many things: enter thou into the joy of thy lord."* You will hear the painful eternal words, *"I never knew you: depart from me you that work iniquity."* And then you will drop off into hell. The things that you are doing you are doing to glorify yourself and not Jesus Christ. When you have a relationship with someone you seek to please him or her. You deny yourself to please the one you love. In **Matthew 16:24-26** it says, *"²⁴Then said Jesus unto his disciples, If any [man] will come after me, let him deny himself, and take up his cross, and follow me.*

²⁵For whosoever will save his life shall lose it: and whosoever will lose his life for my sake shall find it. ²⁶For what is a man profited, if he shall gain the whole world, and lose his own soul? or what shall a man give in exchange for his soul?" When is the last time that you denied yourself to obey Christ? To listen to Him? To praise and worship Him?

What Does It Mean To Have a Relationship

To have a relationship with Jesus Christ we must identify ourselves with Christ. We can know that we have a relationship with Jesus if we are busy allowing the Holy Spirit to do the following things in your life:

(1) By Making Proper Confession of Sins

This is recognition that Christ died on the cross to atone for our sins and that they were actually borne by Him. When we confess that we are sinners and that He bore our sins on the cross we therefore identify ourselves with Him in His work of atonement and cleansing from all sin follows immediately **(1 John 1:9)**.

(2) By Crucifying the Old Man

The old man, as we have known, is the spirit and nature of the devil working in us before we are saved from sin. The old man or the devil constantly works to regain dominion over us after we are saved, so we must be on guard and refuse to give place to the devil **(Eph. 4:27; 5:10-18; James 4:7; 1 Pet. 5:8-9)**. Just because the devil seeks dominion and we are tempted to yield to sin is no sign that we have the old man in us, or that we are in union with the spirit and nature of Satan. It is only when we yield to sin again that we are in harmony **with the devil.**

By the crucifixion of the old man we simply mean that we recognize that we are freed from him and we no longer obey him in any respect. We must consider ourselves dead to him and that he is dead to us. Paul says, *"How shall we that are DEAD TO SIN, live any longer therein? Knowing this that our old man was crucified with him, that the body of sin might be destroyed, that HENCE FORTH WE SHOULD NOT SERVE SIN. For he that is dead is FREED FROM SIN. Now if we be DEAD WITH CHRIST, we believe that we shall LIVE WITH HIM. Knowing that Christ being raised from the dead dieth no more; death hath no more dominion over him. For in that he died, he died unto sin ONCE: but in that he liveth, HE LIVETH UNTO GOD. LIKEWISE RECKON, ye ourselves to be DEAD UNTO SIN, but ALIVE UNTO GOD through Jesus Christ our Lord. Let NOT sin therefore reign in your mortal body, that ye should obey it in the lusts thereof. Neither yield yourselves as instruments of unrighteousness UNTO SIN: but yield yourselves UNTO GOD, as those that are alive from the dead, and your members as instruments of righteousness UNTO GOD. For sin shall not have dominion over you"* **(Rom. 6:1-14)**.

Man must reckon or count himself to be dead to sin and alive to God; that is, he has nothing more to do with sin and everything to do with God. He is to reckon sin as a thing of the past and as non-existent as far as he is concerned. He is to reckon. that God is all and all and the only thing that matters in his life. Just as parents can and sometimes do cast a child out of their home and Cut him off from any further relationship or inheritance, and therefore, as far as they are concerned the child is dead, so the believer must completely give up sin and count that he is dead to it. This can be done by reckoning it done by faith in Christ and by giving one's self wholly over to God and a life of holiness in Christ.

The old man and the whole operation of the devil in life must be ignored and rejected once and for all. The old life, called ***our old man*** who is nothing more or less than the devil working in us, must be done away with and renounced forever. We must reckon that we are new creatures in Christ and the old life dead and that we no longer live as we used to live in sins and lusts that damn the soul. The old life is past and the new life is here. The devil has no more part in us so we reckon him dead (1 John 5:18). The old sins are gone and are counted dead. We are alive to God and we recognize Him as our master. The old life, the old sins, the old man, and the things of the past are still in existence, but as far as we are concerned they are not, because we are dead to them. When we served sin we were dead to God and had no relationship and as far as we were concerned He was not in existence. Now since turning to God and becoming alive to Him we count ourselves to be dead to sin and Satan. One cannot be alive to both. One cannot serve two masters or live two different lives, so when a man or woman is alive to sin he is dead to God and when he is alive to God he is dead to sin. You either have relationship with Jesus or the devil not both. In **Romans 6:16** it says, *"¹⁶Know ye not, that to whom ye yield yourselves servants to obey, his servants ye are to whom ye obey; whether of sin unto death, or of obedience unto righteousness?"*

(3) By Faith in Christ

This includes faith in His name **(Acts 3:16; 4:12)**, faith in His blood **(Rom. 3:24-25), faith in His Word (John 15:7; 2 Cor. 1:20)**, and faith in His death, burial, and resurrection **(Rom. 6:1-8; 1 Cor. 15:1-19)**. We must believe that what Christ died for is ours the moment we accept it. We identify ourselves with Him by faith in all His work and we then have a relationship with Him and receive the benefits for which He died.

(4) By Walking in the Light

"But if we walk in the light, as he is in the light, we have fellowship one with another, and the blood of Jesus Christ his Son cleanseth us FROM ALL SIN" **(John 1:7-9).** This means as we get to know truth we accept it and obey it and it makes us free **(John 8:3 1-32).** This is growing in grace and in the knowledge of God through Jesus Christ **(2 Pet. 1:4-10; 3:18).**

(5) By Taking Up Our Cross Daily to Follow Christ

This means forsaking all that the gospel requires one to give up and loving the Lord with all the heart and soul **(Luke 14:25-27, 33; Matt. 19:27-30).** As one learns truth he must conform to it daily. Whatever the cross may be that we are called upon to bear we must carry it in conformity to the will of God. All selfishness in obeying truth must be denied and the gospel must be obeyed regardless of personal interests **(Mark 8:34-38; 10:23-31).**

(6) By Walking and Living in the Spirit

This means that we seek to know the will of God by the Holy Spirit and the Word of God, and that we shall always follow the leading of the Spirit and reject anything in our lives that would be contrary to the Word of God and our best spiritual interests. We must put to death all the works of the flesh and cultivate the fruit of the Spirit **(Rom. 8:1-16; Gal. 5:16-26; Col. 3:5-17; Jude 20:24; 1 Pet. 1:3-9).**

(7) By Constant Prayer and Study of the Word of God

We know the need of prayer and want to get answers to our prayers. Along with praying there should be constant meditation in the Word of God and a cheerful obedience to it. It is by meditation and study that we get to know the fine points of truth and of spiritual leadings of God. Men and women are required to study **(2 Tim. 2:15)**, search **(John 5:39)**, continue in, and know the truth **(John 8:31-36)**, obey it **(John 14:23-24; Acts 5:32; Rom. 1:5)**, and meditate in it day and night **(Ps. 1; Josh. 1:7-8).** It is by prayer and study and obedience to the Word that faith is increased **(Rom. 10:17)**. We are promised that if the Word abides in us and we abide in Christ we can ask what we will and it shall be done **(John 15:7)**. It is by this that we learn in what ways to identify ourselves with Christ and how to have an intimate relationship with Him.

By Faithful Work for God and Consecration to Help Others

We should realize our responsibility and that we are saved in order for us to serve. We should find the most spiritual church in our community, not necessarily the most popular one, for this latter kind is not always the most spiritual one. We should choose a church that holds up a genuine standard of Christianity and clean holy living according to the gospel. We should go to a church that demands of its members that they live free from sin and the bad habits that will damn the soul It will pay us great dividends here and hereafter to choose wisely the church that will help develop our faith and encourage us in following the whole Bible.

Regardless of what church we go to, we must be sure that we co-operate with the pastor and the program of the church in the winning of lost souls. We should attend every meeting that it is at all possible for us to attend. The Bible says, "*25Not forsaking the assembling of ourselves together, as the manner of some is; but exhorting one another: and so much the more, as ye see the day approaching.*" **(Heb. 10:25)**. We should back our pastor in prayer and be the kind of members that he can depend upon. We should get busy for God and use every opportunity we get to be a witness for Jesus either in public or in private. Never turn down an opportunity to lead prayer meetings, visit the sick, help the needy, or to do religious and social work.

During the next two weeks you should 'spend much time in prayer and in reading the Bible and this book. Study the lessons and consecrate yourself to the best good of all. It is by spiritual exercise that you will grow spiritually. It is by doing your duty to the church and the whole work of the Lord that you will grow in grace and knowledge and become rich in experience and relationship with Jesus Christ.

Give up all wickedness and bad habits. Be temperate and moderate in all things. Be humble in word and deed. Renounce your own will and ways, clinging earnestly to God and your Christian principles and convictions. Be zealous, obedient, and free from murmuring. Constantly remember that you were a sinner and that you are saved by grace and you are what you are only by the grace of God.

Learn to redeem the time and overcome all idleness. Covet no man's goods. Make the best of all that comes your way. Quickly forgive anyone because of any differences. Cultivate purity of body, soul, and spirit. Be gentle and kind to all men. Be truthful and honest in all your dealings. Follow the example of Christ and the simple instructions of the Bible in all things of life, and you will have a great influence for Christ over others and be blessed in all things in life.

If you will study the Bible and believe its promises and follow the simple instructions that we give you, it will be impossible to fail God or to fail to have a relationship with Jesus Christ, get from God the wonderful benefits He has promised. Believe in the reality of sin, sickness, Satan, demons, and God. Learn that the true source of help in life comes from God.

Learn how to pray and what to pray for. Do not be satisfied to live like many so-called Christians around you. Step ahead of the crowd and be an example to others and never stumble over anyone. If you stumble over one hypocrite he is ahead of you or you would not stumble over him.

Practice constantly the presence of God and overcome sin and bad habits. Believe that you can have healing and health and all the things promised by God. Seek God daily to attain to these benefits and your life will be blessed beyond anything that you now realize.

Now you will have a dynamic relationship with Jesus Christ and if Satan bothers you *"TAKE SATAN TO COURT."*

Summing It All Up
Galatians 2:20

²⁰I am crucified with Christ: nevertheless I live; yet not I, but Christ liveth in me: and the life which I now live in the flesh I live by the faith of the Son of God, who loved me, and gave himself for me.

The chief secret of all redemptive benefits is man's identification with Christ in His work for fallen man. By identification with Christ we mean our union with or relationship with Him in all phases of His redemptive work. Do we have religion or relationship. It says in **Matthew 15:8**, "*⁸This people draweth nigh unto me with their mouth, and honoureth me with [their] lips; but their heart is far from me.*" Everyone who believes in Christ must become identified WITH him in every phase of His life, death, burial, resurrection, and manifestation. Believers are spoken of as being identified WITH Christ in:

1. **His sufferings** (Rom. 8:17; 1 Pet. 4:1-2; John 15:20; 16:2-3; Matt. 10:25).
2. **His work** (Mark 16:20; John 14:12-15; Heb. 2:3-4; Acts 1:1-2; Matt. 28:19-20).
3. **His crucifixion** (Rom. 6:6; 8:12-13; Gal. 2:20; Col. 3:5-17).
4. **His death** (Rom. 6:3-11; 8:17; 1 Pet. 4:1-2; Col. 3:3).
5. **His burial** (Rom. 6:4; Col. 2:12).
6. **His resurrection** (Rom. 6:5; Col. 2:12; 3:1; Eph. 2:5-6).
7. **His exaltation. and glory** (Rom. 8:17; Col. 3:4; Eph. 2:5-6).
8. **His security** (Col. 3:1-4; 1 Thess. 4:16-17).

CHAPTER SIXTEEN

You Can Be Part Of The Family Today

WHAT IS A CHRISTIAN?

A real Christian is any man, woman, or child who comes to God as a lost sinner, accepts the Lord Jesus Christ as Their Personal Savior, surrenders to Him as their Lord and Master, confesses Him as such before the world, and strives to please Him in everything every day of their life.

Have YOU come to God realizing that you are a lost sinner? Have YOU accepted the Lord Jesus Christ as YOUR personal Savior? Do YOU believe with all your heart like **Isa. 53:5-6** said, *that God laid all YOUR iniquity on Him,* and that according to **Pet 2:24**, *He bore YOUR sins and the penalty of YOUR sins, and that YOUR sins are forgiven now because Jesus died in YOUR stead?*

Have **YOU** surrendered to Him as your Lord and Master? Are YOU willing to do His will even when it conflicts with your desires? Have YOU confessed to Him that YOU are a sinner; that you believe HE bore the penalty of **YOUR** sins, and that therefore YOU confess **Him** as **YOUR** Saviour and Master before the world?

Is it YOUR determination to strive to please Him in everything, every day of **YOUR** life? If you can sincerely answer "**YES**" to the foregoing questions, then you may know on the authority of God's Word that YOU are NOW a child of God **(John 1:12)**, that YOU have NOW eternal life **(John 3:36)**. If you have done **YOUR** part to believe that Christ died in **YOUR** place, and have received Him by faith as **YOUR** Saviour and Master, then you can be sure that God has done His pert and impelled to you His own nature. In **2 Pet 1:4,** it says "*⁴Whereby are given unto us exceeding great and precious promises: that by these ye might be partaker of the divine nature, having escaped the corruption that is in the world through lust.*"

But if you are not yet sure that you have personally accepted the Lord Jesus Christ into your heart as your Saviour, and if you have not yet definitely surrendered your life to Him and publicly confessed Him as your Lord and Master, then nothing gives me more joy than to point you the way to peace with God, forgiveness of sins and to the great joy of Christian living. Consider the following carefully.

SALVATION IS A SERIOUS MATTER

These 7 steps of instructions are for the use of those who have a serious desire to obtain the mercy of God, which alone can deliver them from their evil habits, from the power of the devil, and from eternal hell. To those who will consider and obey them, I give the following counsel:

(1) Set apart a special time for their consideration retiring, if possible, into some quiet place where you can be alone with God.

(2) Read the 7 steps carefully and thoughtfully from the first to the last, and then go through them again.

(3) Earnestly pray for that guidance of the Holy Spirit which God has promised to all who seek Him.

(4) With all your heart, on your knees before God, take one step at a time. Be careful not to leave the first step for the second until

it is clearly understood, heartily accepted, and solemnly decided upon; and so on with the second and third steps, until the last is reached.

(5) If this course be followed, I feel very sure that no sincere person will fail to reach not only the mercy-seat of grace, but the loving arms of the Saviour, the knowledge of the forgiveness of his sins, and of present salvation.

FIRST STEP

Admit You Are A Sinner.

"*²³For ALL have sinned and come short of the glory of God*" **(Romans 3:23).**

"*⁸If we say that we have no sin, we deceive ourselves*" **(1 John 1:8).**

I am a sinner. I have sinned against my God, against my neighbor, and against my own soul. I have sinned in my thoughts, in my feelings, in my conversation, and in my action. I have sinned at home, in my family, and I have sinned in the world, in my business and pleasures. I have done the things I ought not to have done. I freely admit it. I will not cover my sins. They have been more in number than I can count, and grievous beyond the possibility of calculation. They have dishonored my heavenly Father, treated the sacrifice of my Saviour with contempt, exercised a bad influence upon the members of my own family, and upon those who have known me in the world. I deserve the everlasting displeasure of God, and I see that if I die in my sins I shall fall into the damnation of hell. O Lord, have mercy upon me!

SECOND STEP

Be Sorry For Your Sin.

"*¹³And the publican, standing afar off, would not lift up so much as his eyes unto heaven, but SMOTE UPON HIS BREAST, saying, GOD BE MERCIFUL TO ME A SINNER*" **(Luke 18:13).**

"*¹⁰For godly SORROW worketh repentance to salvation*" **(2 Cor. 7:10).**

Not only so I see that I have sinned against God, but I am truly sorry for having done so, I hate my evil habits, and I hate that I followed them. I am grieved on account of my sins, not only because they have been committed against my heavenly Father who has continually loved and cared for me, If I could undo the past, gladly would I do so, but I cannot, The sins I have committed are written down against me in the Book of God's remembrance. No prayers that I can offer, no tears that I can shed, no lamentations that I make, no good works that I can perform will remove that terrible record. My only hope is in the forgiving mercy of Jesus Christ; who has said, "*³⁷Him that cometh to Me, I will in no wise cast out*" **(John 6:37).**

THIRD STEP

Confess Your Sin To God.

"*¹³He that covereth his sins shall not prosper: but whoso CONFESSETH AND FORSAKETH them shall have mercy*" **(Proverbs 28:13).**

"*⁹If we CONFESS our sins, He is faithful and just to forgive us our sins, and to cleanse us from all unrighteousness*" **(1 John 1:9).**

Not only am I sorry on account of my sins and bad habits, but I freely confess and acknowledge them before God. I have no excuse to make for them. It may be true that much of the evil of which I have been guilty had been done in ignorance. I did not know God, nor my duty to Him, nor the greatness of the love of my Saviour in dying for me. I was ignorant of the evil influence which my bad habits and sins were often exercising on others. But this ignorance is no real excuse, because I should have known better. I ought to have read my Bible and listened to those who would have taught me. I ought to have thought about my soul and cried to God for help, but I did not, and, consequently, my heart was not open before Him. And I do here and now confess myself before God to be a guilty sinner, without excuse, deserving His anger now and forever.

Not only do I make this confession in private to God, but seeing that I have sinned in the presence of my family and of the people around me, l am perfectly willing to confess my sinfulness, and my sorrow on account of it, as far as I have the opportunity, before the Lord's people, before my own family, and before the world. Not having been ashamed to sin in the presence of others, l am willing to acknowledge it in their presence.

FOURTH STEP

Putting Away Sin Before God.

"*⁷Let the wicked FORSAKE HIS WAY, and the unrighteous man his thoughts: and let him return unto the Lord, and He will have mercy upon him... for he will abundantly pardon*" **(Isaiah 55:7)**.

Not only do I see myself to be a sinner, and hate my sins and habits confess them before God and man, but I do now, by God's help, renounce and give up every one of them. Whatever pleasure they may have brought me in the pest; and whatever earthly gain they may promise me in the future, I do here and now, in the strength of God, put them away, and promise with the Holy Spirit help that I will never take them back again.

FIFTH STEP

Asking God Forgiveness for Sin.

"*Who FORGIVETH ALL thine iniquities*" **(Psalms 103:3)**.

"*¹⁸Come now, let us reason together, saith the Lord: though your sins be as scarlet, they shall be white as snow; though they be red like crimson, they shall be as wool*" **(Isa. 1:18)**. Feeling how shamefully I have rebelled against my heavenly Father in despising His love, in breaking His commandments, and in influencing others to do the same, I do here and now, on my knees, submit myself to Him, humbly praying that He will have mercy upon me, a miserable sinner, and begging Him for Christ's sake to forgive all my sins, to receive me into His favor, and to make me, unworthy as I am, a member of His family.

SIXTH STEP

Consecrate Yourself to God.

"*³²Whosoever therefore shall CONFESS ME BEFORE MEN, him will I confess also before My Father which is in heaven*" (Matt 10:32).

"⁹But ye are a chosen generation, a royal priesthood an holy nation, a peculiar people; that ye should SHEW FORTH THE PRAISE 011 HIM who hath called you out of darkness into His marvelous light" **(1 Peter 2:9).**

I promise God, here and now, in His strength, and with all my heart; that if He will forgive me and receive me into His favor, I will from this time engage to be His faithful servant, promising to spend the rest of my days in doing what I can for His glory, for the extension of His kingdom, and for the salvation of those around me.

SEVENTH STEP
Have Faith In God For Salvation.

"⁸For by grace are ye shaved, THROUGH FAITH; and that not of yourselves; it is the gift of God: ⁹Not of works, lest any man should boast" **(Eph. 2:8-9).**

I believe that Jesus Christ, Good's Son, in His great mercy and love died for me and in my place, bearing my sins in His own body on the cross. And believing this, I do here and now welcome Him to my heart as my Saviour from hell, from sin, from wicked habits and from the power of the devil. I accept Him as Lord of my life, and here and now devote my life to pleasing Him. Jesus Christ says in the Bible that if I will come to Him, He will in nowise cast me out; and I so come to Him with all my heart just now, as a poor, helpless, guilty sinner, seeking salvation, and trusting only in His blood. I am sure that He does not reject me. I believe that He does at this very moment take me in. He was bruised for my iniquities; the punishment I ought to have endured was laid upon Him, and He bore it for me. I know I am forgiven now. Praise the Lord! Jesus saves me now!

FULFILL ALL RIGHTEOUSNESS BEFORE GOD

"¹⁵And Jesus answering said unto him, Suffer it to be so now: For thus it becometh us to fulfil ALL RIGHTEOUSNESS" **(Matt 3:15).**

Now that YOU have become a child of God, the success and growth of YOUR Christian life depends on yourself. The blessing of every real Christian life in his own community is beyond description. When others will refuse to read the Bible, your life will be read by them daily. To the end that you will live a useful and joyful Christian life, and so bring blessing to all about you, I have prepared the following suggestions. Read them carefully and practice them daily until they become a part of your own life or in other words, until they become habitual. Through brief, they are of vital importance, and they will be treasured by you throughout life's journey, and will produce untold blessings in the lives of thousands of others who watch you.

STUDY THE BIBLE

Set aside at least fifteen minutes a day for Bible study. Let God talk to you fifteen minutes a day through His Word. You talk to God fifteen minutes a day in prayer. Then talk for Cod fifteen minutes a day in testifying and personal witnessing to others. In **1 Peter 2:2** it says, *"²As newborn babes, desire the sincere milk of the Word, that ye may grow thereby."* The word of God is food for the soul. In Matthew 4:4 it says, *"⁴But he [Jesus] answered and said, It is written, Man shall not live by bread alone but by every word that proceedeth out of the mouth of God."* Commit to memory one verse of scripture each day. In **Psalms 119:11** it says, *"¹¹Thy Word have I hid in mine heart, that I might not sin against thee."* Join a good Bible class.

PRAY MUCH

Praying is talking to God. Talk to Him about everything, Your perplexities, joys, sorrows, sin, mistakes, friends, enemies and your bad habits. Talk to Him as you would talk to your own father. Talk to Him in your everyday manner of language. In **Phil. 4:6** it says, *"⁶Be careful for nothing, but in everything by prayer and supplication with thanksgiving, let your requests be made known unto God."*

WIN SOMEONE FOR CHRIST

For spiritual growth you need not only food (Bible study), but exercise. Work for Christ. The work Christ gave us is to win others. In **Mark 16:15** it says, *"¹⁵Go into all the world and preach the gospel to every creature."* In **Ezekiel 3:18** it says, *"¹⁸When I say unto the wicked, thou shalt surely die; and thou gives him not warning, nor speakest to* *warn the wicked from his wicked way, to save his life; the same wicked man shall die in his iniquity; but his blood will I require at thine hand."* If they are sick, pray for them. **(Read Matt 25:31-46.)** In **Mark 16:18** it says, *"¹⁸These signs shall follow them that believe they shall lay hands on the sick, and they shall recover."*

SHUN EVIL COMPANIONS

Avoid bad people, bad books, and bad thoughts, bad movies on T.V. because they will surely lead to bad habits. In **2 Cor. 6:14-15;17** it says, *"¹⁴Be ye not unequally yoked together with unbelievers: For what fellowship hath righteousness with unrighteousness? and what communion hath light with darkness? ... ¹⁵What part hath he that believeth with an infidel? ¹⁷Wherefore come out from among them, and be ye separate, saith the Lord."* Try to win the wicked for God, but do not choose them for your company and companions.

JOIN SOME GOOD CHURCH

Be sure that the church you join believes and teaches the blood of Jesus Christ to wash away sins, and the stripes of Jesus Christ to heal our diseases; be sure that it is a church whose doctrine agrees with the contents of the Word of God. Be faith in your attendance to all the church services as much as is within your will to do so. In **Hebrews 10:25** it says, *"²⁵Not forsaking the assembling of ourselves together, as the manner of some is."* Cooperate with your pastor. God has appointed the pastor to be a shepherd over the church and you should give him due respect and seek to assist him in every plan to further the cause of Christ in that church. In **Hebrews 13:17** it says, *"¹⁷Obey them that have the rule over you, and submit yourselves: for they watch for your souls, as they that must give account, that they may do it with joy, and not with grief: for that [is] unprofitable for you."*

CHAPTER SEVENTEEN
IT'S A WAKE-UP CALL FOR CHRISTIANS

Titus 2:14

"¹⁴Who gave himself for us, that he might redeem us from all iniquity, and purify unto himself a peculiar people, zealous of good works."

We Must Fully Commit

As Christians we must show a high capacity for adjustment. Shoot for instant alignment. Take personal responsibility for adapting to change. We must commit fully to Jesus Christ and expect Him to expect more from each of us as Christians. Jesus wants a much better quality in service than we have ever given before. He wants high performance Christians. Better service calls for highly committed Christians. We should not waste energy resisting change, and killing precious time like chickens sitting on the nest hatching self-pity eggs. Either buy in or buy out, because that's best for the whole Body of Christ. In **1 Kings 18:21** it says,

"*²¹And Elijah came unto all the people, and said, How long halt ye between two opinions? if the LORD [be] God, follow him: but if Baal, [then] follow him. And the people answered him not a word.*" Jesus Christ wants strong committed Christians and he will not settle for anything less. Being a strong committed Christian empowers us, bring out our best talents and Potential, build up the Whole Body of Christ and makes us more valuable workers in the service of God. Commitment is for sure the quality that we must have and cultivate in order to join, march, and fight with this army of born-again, blood bought, baptized, Holy Ghost filled believers.

Watch Our Time
Ephesians 5:16-17

"*¹⁶Redeeming the time, because the days are evil.*

¹⁷Wherefore be ye not unwise, but understanding what the will of the Lord [is]."

We need to redeem the time and operate with a strong sense of urgency. We need to accelerate in all aspects of our Christian work. The emphasize is on "**action.**" Being about Jesus business. Don't wait until you are perfect before you make a move, you may never move. Learn to correct mistakes dynamically as you move in the direction of perfection not let them cause you to become static and stop your all forward motion altogether. Learn to make mistakes, correct them repent, **(1 John 1:9)** and press on. Seek radical breakthrough, quantum leaps in the utilization and management of your time. Take no part whatsoever in habits, people and things that waste your time and cause you to resist change through the Holy Spirit.

Conform To Jesus Image
Romans 8:29

"*²⁹For whom he did foreknow, he also did predestinate [to be] conformed to the image of his Son, that he might be the firstborn among many brethren.*"

See yourself being conformed to the image of Jesus Christ. Create role clarity for yourself. Practice personality analysis projection. Take personal responsibility for learning God's will and purpose for your life, then propels yourself in that direction. Don't draw back, waiting for someone else to hold your hand and lead you along. Chase down the information you need. Seek and you shall find, knock and the door will be open, ask and it shall be given unto you. Show initiative in getting your bearing, and in aligning your efforts with God's larger plans.

Become A Team Player
Romans 12:10 Psalms 133:1

"[Be] kindly affectioned one to another with brotherly love; in honour preferring one another; A Song of degrees of David. Behold, how good and how pleasant [it is] for brethren to dwell together in unity!"

Behave like you are really part of the team. Jesus Christ wants us to act like his ambassadors in the earth. More power, information and responsibility need to flow through us. We need to assume more personal responsibility for success of God's work in the earth, rather than focusing narrowly within the boundaries of our own little groups and denominations. After all Jesus have only **"ONE"** Body in the earth. We need to operate from a position of knowledge, wisdom, power, and understanding. Consider how you personally can help build up the Kingdom of God in the earth, serve each other better, and improve your art of fishing in lost souls, in a wicked, evil, and dying world.

Become Accountable For The Outcome
2 Timothy 2:15

"[15]Study to shew thyself approved unto God, a workman that needeth not to be ashamed, rightly dividing the word of truth."

Know your subject. Study to show yourself approved. The Godhead takes no pleasure in Christians that gets lazy about learning. Either you take personal responsibility for continuing your spiritual education or you will end up without the knowledge you need to wage a successful spiritual warfare against the Devil. You should invest in your own growth, spiritual development, and self-renewal, so that you can offer better service to Jesus Christ.

Praying, meditating and studying own your own should become a regular part of your daily routine as much as eating. Not only receiving a snack once a week.

Hold yourself accountable for outcomes and stop blaming God if your prayers are not answered. Jesus has already done whatever he needed to do to make us successful. God through Jesus Christ has given us the knowledge of everything that pertains to life and Godliness, **(2 Pet 1:3)** and we are complete through Jesus our Lord **(Col. 2:10)**. The Godhead is insisting on new levels of accountability in Christian responsibility, power, and authority. Therefore we must stand accountable for the results. We are Free Moral Agents, self-directed spirits and empowered souls. Holding ourselves personally accountable for the outcome requires that we think broadly, know the truth about us, and consider the big picture. Look beyond ourselves and immediate needs to see if we are doing all that we can do to bring about the right results for the Glory of God through Jesus Christ Our Lord. We should understand how our prayers, life-styles, approach to problems, attitude and behavior can interfere with the outcome of our mission and goals.

Add To Your Account

Philippians 4:17

"[17]Not because I desire a gift: but I desire fruit that may abound to your account."

There will be payday someday. Rewards are being added to your account. But you don't get rewarded for just "putting in your time on earth," You get rewarded for performance. Make a difference, add enough value so that everyone can see that something very special would be missing if you went home to be with the Lord. The question was asked, **"If they came to arrest you for being a Christian, would there be enough evidence to convict you?"** Are you sending up fruit that may abound to your account daily.

Become A Service Center
Luke 22:26

"²⁶But ye shall not be so: but he that is greatest among you, let him be as the younger; and he that is chief, as he that doth serve."

Jesus came to serve, not only to be served. See yourself as a service center. We need an in-depth feeling and compassion for those we serve. What do our customer need, and how do we fit into the picture? What does it take to help them? How can we contribute to their success? We must get close, intimately close to our customers. Seek regular, direct contact with them. Build a strong relationship. Deliver the highest quality service possible. Anticipate their needs, and develop a reputation for responsiveness. Talk like Jesus talked, walk as Jesus walked, do as Jesus did, and love as Jesus loved. Then we will experience what Jesus experienced. How often do you visit the sick, feed the poor etc. Jesus said in **Matt. 25:35**, *"³⁵For I was an hungred, and ye gave me meat: I was thirsty, and ye gave me drink: I was a stranger, and ye took me in: Naked, and ye clothed me: I was sick, and ye visited me: I was in prison, and ye came unto me."* How many times have you left the 99 and gone after the one that you haven't seen in church lately? In **Matt. 18:12**, *"¹²How think ye? if a man have an hundred sheep, and one of them be gone astray, doth he not leave the ninety and nine, and goeth into the mountains, and seeketh that which is gone astray?"*

Don't Let Your Joy Get Stolen
John 15:11

"¹¹These things have I spoken unto you, that my joy might remain in you, and [that] your joy might be full."

Keep your spirits high. People will not always respond to you the way that you want them to because of lack of knowledge and understanding. Manage your own morale. Keep joy in your heart and a spring in your step. Don't worry be happy. Don't put anyone else in charge of your morale, if you do you will disempower yourself. If you wait around for someone else to heal your wounded spirit, you will end up hurting longer than necessary. We must assume personal responsibility for our own attitude control. Don't let low morale drain away precious energy, destroy your self-confidence and maybe your testimony for Jesus Christ. Take charge of your moods, bounce back, be tough skinned and get you emotions under control. Christ said that if we would suffer for Him we would also reign with Him. In **2 Timothy 2:12,** *"¹²If we suffer, we shall also reign with [him]: if we deny [him], he also will deny us."* We must do all that we do to the glory of God. We will all carry some battle scars in the war between good and evil.

Practice A Holy Walk

1 Peter 1:15

"¹⁵But as he which hath called you is holy, so be ye holy in all manner of conversation"

Practice Holiness. The Body of Christ can't improve unless Christians does. Holiness requires continuous improvement. Think of it as the daily pursuit of excellence. Holiness keeps us reaching, stretching and looking upward in order to be better today than we were yesterday. The continuous improvements may come bit by bit, line upon line, and precept upon precepts, but enough of these incremental gains will eventually add up to a holy walk that will please God. Every single Christian should assume personal responsibility for upgrading his or her Christian performance. Our Christian walk, service, attitude, behavior and power should all show steady gains since we were born again. Our skills in fighting the spiritual warfare and pulling down strongholds should be in a constant renewal and review. There should be a drive toward an ever-improving performance in our Christian walk.

Be the Solution to Problems

Philippians 2:3-4

"³[Let] nothing [be done] through strife or vainglory; but in lowliness of mind let each esteem other better than themselves. ⁴Look not every man on his own things, but every man also on the things of others."

We must be the solution and not the problem. Be a problem fixer and not a finger pointer because when you point one finger at someone else you have four pointing back at you. Problems are the natural offspring of change and daily living. We must be able to take care of problems, not merely point them out. We should seek to be known as a problem solver not a problem causer.

We must remember that we have a common enemy. In **Eph. 6:12** it says, *"*^{12}*For we wrestle not against flesh and blood, but against principalities, against powers, against the rulers of the darkness of this world, against spiritual wickedness in high [places]."* You see we need each other because a house that is divided against itself cannot stand. In **Mark 3:25** it says, *"*^{25}*And if a house be divided against itself, that house cannot stand. And if Satan rise up against himself, and be divided, he cannot stand, but hath an end."* Peace, cooperation and unity is what we need in the body of Christ. In **Eph. 4:3-6** it says, *"*^{3}*Endeavouring to keep the unity of the Spirit in the bond of peace. *^{4}*[There is] one body, and one Spirit, even as ye are called in one hope of your calling; *^{5}*One Lord, one faith, one baptism, *^{6}*One God and Father of all, who [is] above all, and through all, and in you all."*

The Christian charge

My fellow brother and sister in Christ, this is indeed a wakeup call for Christian. Jesus said that He would come as a thief in the night. In **1 Thess. 5:2-11** it says, *"*^{2}*For yourselves know perfectly that the day of the Lord so cometh as a thief in the night. *^{3}*For when they shall say, Peace and safety; then sudden destruction cometh upon them, as travail upon a woman with child; and they shall not escape. *^{4}*But ye, brethren, are not in darkness, that that day should overtake you as a thief. *^{5}*Ye are all the children of light, and the children of the day: we are not of the night, nor of darkness. *^{6}*Therefore let us not sleep, as [do] others; but let us watch and be sober. *^{7}*For they that sleep sleep in the night; and they that be drunken are drunken in the night. *^{8}*But let us, who are of the day, be sober, putting on the breastplate of faith and love; and for an helmet, the hope of salvation. *^{9}*For God hath not appointed us to wrath, but to obtain salvation by our Lord Jesus Christ, *^{10}*Who died for us, that, whether we wake or sleep, we should live together with him.*

¹¹*Wherefore comfort yourselves together, and edify one another, even as also ye do."*

He also said in **Matt. 16:2-3,** *"²He answered and said unto them, When it is evening, ye say, [It will be] fair weather: for the sky is red. ³And in the morning, [It will be] foul weather to day: for the sky is red and lowering. O [ye] hypocrites, <u>ye can discern the face of the sky; but can ye not [discern] the signs of the times</u>?"* Are you watching, serving, and waiting for the Lords eminent return?

CHAPTER EIGHTEEN

IN SUMMARY WE ARE IN SPIRITUAL WARFARE NOW NOW!!!!!!

Spiritual warfare mean just what it **says "Spiritual warfare."** You cannot see with your physical eyes whom you are fighting, they are spiritual. Although they can manifest themselves where they can be seen if they so desire. But normally they keep out of the sight of the average human being and do their dirty work. This presents a fearful awesome problem to human beings. We can't fight what we can't see. We can only know about them and how to fight them by using the **"Word of God."** It says in **2 Cor. 5:7**, *"For we walk by faith, not by sight."* The difference between spiritual warfare and physical warfare is tremendous. In physical warfare you can at least see you enemy, buy the same or better weapons than he has and use your own might and power to kill, reduce in size, defeat or even destroy your enemy. The enemy in spiritual warfare are more powerful, quicker, more intelligent, and more numerous than the human being by themselves and they can never die or be killed by human effort. But with the **"Word of God"** which is Jesus Christ we can defeat the strongest enemy even Satan himself. We are encouraged, bold and confidence about what we read in the Bible in **Rev. 12:11,** *"¹¹And they overcame him by the blood of the Lamb, and by the word of their testimony..."* Also we are told in **1 John 3:8,** *"⁸He that committeth sin is of the devil; for the devil sinneth from the beginning. For this purpose the Son of God was manifested, that he might destroy the works of the devil."*

You must be aware of the fact that spiritual warfare is very different than physical warfare because we are forced to exercise faith. It says in **Heb. 11:1,** *"Now faith is the substance of things hoped for, the evidence of things not seen."* As we put our faith and trust in Jesus Christ He will give us the victory. It says in **1 John 5:4-5,** *"⁴For whatsoever is born of God overcometh the world: and this is the victory that overcometh the world, [even] our faith. ⁵Who is he that overcometh the world, but he that believeth that Jesus is the Son of God?"*

Even though we cannot see the real enemy and opponent whom we are fighting against, our eyes are opened and the vail is taken away through faith in God through Jesus Christ. It says in **Ephesians 6:12,** *"¹²For we wrestle not against flesh and blood, but against principalities, against powers, against the rulers of the darkness of this world, against spiritual wickedness in high [places]."*

Warfare is the waging of war against an enemy. It is an armed conflict undertaken to destroy or undermine the strength of another. The Bible says, in **2 Corinthians 10:4-5,** *"⁴For the weapons of our warfare [are] not carnal, but mighty through God to the pulling down of strong holds;) ⁵Casting down imaginations, and every high thing that exalteth itself against the knowledge of God, and bringing into captivity every thought to the obedience of Christ."* Spiritual warfare is not fought using weapons such as our hands, guns, knives, nuclear weapons, or any of these conventional weapons. Not even the most power physical weapon on the face of the earth will do. No matter what weapons are used spiritual or physical the goal is still the same. The Word of God tells us what our enemy come to do to us and it also tell us what our ally come to do for us in **John 10:10** it says, *"¹⁰The thief cometh not, but for to steal, and to kill, and to destroy:*

I am come that they might have life, and that they might have [it] more abundantly". Jesus is our ally, helper, and savior. In **1 John 3:8** it says, "*⁸He that committeth sin is of the devil; for the devil sinneth from the beginning. For this purpose the Son of God was manifested, that he might destroy the works of the devil.*" We are no match for our enemy Satan, that is why Jesus warns us in **John 15:5**, "*...for without me ye can do nothing.*" As we have shown throughout this book that Jesus is the only match for Satan. With Jesus help we can successfully take Satan to the Supreme Court of God and win.

Who Is Satan in Summary?

According to **Isa. 14:12-14; Ezek. 28:11-17; Luke 10:18; 2 Pet. 3:4-8; Jer. 4:23-26**; and other passages. Satan, known as Lucifer, had a kingdom on the Earth long before the six days of **Gen. 1:3-2:25** and the creation of Adam. These passages reveal that he, through pride, fell and led an invasion against Heaven and was defeated. At that time the Earth was cursed, and the first flood, as in **Gen. 1:2** destroyed all life.

How long Lucifer ruled the Earth in perfect harmony with the kingdom of God is not known, but it was for a long period, for it took a long time to work up such a rebellion as he did. He caused over one-third of God's own angels to rebel, as well as all his own earthly subjects **(Rev. 12:3-4)**.

He regained dominion over the Earth in Adam's day and usurped man's dominion by causing the fall of man and by being the stronger of two sets of rebels after Adam sinned. Adam submitted to Lucifer who got the upper hand of all human rebels because he had the power of sin and death. When Adam fell there were only two human rebels, but opposing them there were innumerable fallen angels and demons. Naturally the stronger set of rebels would come to dominate the weaker, and this is what happened in the case of the spirit and human rebels on the Earth. If man had not fallen he would have been able to overcome them, and they never could have regained dominion over the Earth; but when man sinned, he became powerless against the many spirit rebels and fell under their control.

Man lost the power he had with God and severed partnerships with the Creator therefore could not cope with so many and more powerful spirit rebels. It is only as man lays down his arms of rebellion against God and regains the favor of the Creator and partnership with Him by the new birth that he will be able to have power over these fallen spirit rebels. This is why the new birth and the full surrender to God the Enduement of power is necessary before man can conquer and cast out demons and destroy all the works of the devil. Satan's relationship to man through the various ages has been that of a usurper of man's dominion; and as long as man tolerates his dictatorship over him, that long will he remain subject to him in the individual life. Each man now can, by the power of the gospel, defeat Satan and get rid of all demon relationship in his own life. This is what God demands, and He has provided the means whereby it can be attained.

Man no longer needs to be defeated and always be sick, sinful, helpless, unhappy, and poverty-stricken. Although man cannot get rid of Satan's present power over his dominion by himself except as an individual who will meet the conditions of the gospel, man's dominion can be fully restored to him when the Messiah comes. Then Satan's present position ruler of this world's system and as prince of this world will be ended forever. In **2 Cor. 4:4** it says, "*⁴In whom the god of this world hath blinded the minds of them which believe not, lest the light of the glorious gospel of Christ, who is the image of God, should shine unto them.*"

Man will again inherit the Earth and will live again in the Earth forever as before the fall. Satan's dominion is forcing its rule upon men by sheer force of power. This power will be broken, and Satan will have but three and one-half more years to rule the Earth in the war in Heaven of **Rev. 12:7-14** is ended.

The Methods That Satan Uses in Fighting Spiritual Warfare

Satan uses every conceivable method and means to keep men from God and in subjection to himself. If he fails to do this, he tries to kill the believer's testimony and ruin his influence for God. If one falls he tries to cause him to commit suicide or stay fallen.

He tries to get others in a lukewarm condition and make them live there so that God will cut them off in the end. In **Rev. 3:16** it says, *"¹⁶So then because thou art lukewarm, and neither cold nor hot, I will spew thee out of my mouth."*

He brings in damnable heresies to lead men in rebellion against God **(2 Pet. 2:1-2; 1 Tim. 4:1-8)**. He preaches sermons and uses all the influences possible through fallen men, fallen angels, and demons to get men to stay away from God, or cause them to backslide and live in sin. He is the author of all false religions and never discourages men in following them, for he knows this is one way that is sure to damn their souls.

He tries to cause men to end their lives by making them think that is the best way out, but he hides the true fact that this will be only the beginning of real torment in eternal Hell. He dares men to do many things that they would not do under ordinary circumstances, and men are foolish enough to think they are not brave if they do not accept his dares. He makes the young people think they are missing everything in life if they do not go into all kinds of sins that will damn their souls. He points out to them the glamour of sin and pleasure. He stirs unholy passions in them and causes them to throw away all restraint and live a life of revelry. He makes them think there is no joy in serving the Lord. This is one of his greatest errors. Serving Christ and winning souls that will be thankful forever pays the greatest dividends and affords the greatest pleasures of all existence. Young people should get right with God and taste the glories of salvation; then they will not listen to Satan; they will not go into sin and shame.

Satan preaches to the businessman that he needs to take all his time to get rich before serving the Lord, while the fact is that if any man will truly serve the Lord, he can be abundantly prosperous by God's help. It says in **Matt. 16:26**, *"²⁶For what is a man profited, if he shall gain the whole world, and lose his own soul? or what shall a man give in exchange for his soul?"* He tries to get churches and their leaders to make religion a paying proposition and appeal to the rich and the influential people, to make salvation easy for all, to lower the standards of the Bible on holy living, to become formal and outward in Christian worship and living, to compromise the essentials of the faith, to preach current events and have book reviews in the pulpit instead of preaching the gospel that will save the soul, to justify the sins and unholy lives of church members and to be as much like the world as possible in order to attract the world.

There is no realm which Satan does not seek to control, and he will never be satisfied until as many of his dupes as possible are in eternal Hell and God is defeated and prevented from blessing all men everywhere with all the good things of life. He has greatly succeeded in getting men in all walks of life to give up Christ and the Bible by the excuse that there are so many religions that one cannot tell what to do or which one is right.

He is the deceiver of all men and women **(Rev. 12:9; 20:1-10; 2 Cor. 11:14)**. He had the power of death until Christ conquered death, Hell, and the grave **(Heb. 2:14; Rev. 12:11)**. He is the leader of all sinners and backsliders in the human race **(1 John 3:8; 1 Tim. 5:15)** and of all spirit rebels **(Eph. 6:10-18; Matt. 9:34)**. He causes all sickness and diseases and physical and mental maladies in the human race **(Luke 13:16; John 10:38)**. He takes advantage of all adversities of men to further their rebellion and hold them captive **(2 Cor. 2:11; 1 Tim 1:20; 5:11-15)**.

He tempts men **(Mark 1:13; 1 Cor. 7:5)**; provokes to sin **(1 Chr. 21:1)**; causes disease **(Matt. 16:23)**; transforms himself into an angel of light **(2 Cor. 11:14)**; causes resistance **(Zech. 3:1-2)**; enters into union with others against God **(Luke 22:3)**; sends messengers to defeat saints **(2 Cor. 12:1)**; hinders the gospel **(Romans 2:8; Acts 13:10)**; steals the Word of God from people lest they should believe **(Matt. 13:19; Luke 8:12)**; works miracles **(2 Thess. 2:9)**; contends with messengers of God and sometimes holds them captive **(Dan. 10:12-21; Jude 9)**; hinders believers prayer **(Dan. 10:12-21)**; sets snares for men to fall into sin **(1 Tim. 3:7; 2 Tim. 1:26)**; makes war on the saints **(Eph. 6:10-18)**; causes diversions and blinds men to the gospel **(2 Cor. 4:4)**; causes double mindedness **(Jas. 1:5-9)**; causes doubt and unbelief **(Rom. 14:23; Gen. 3:4-5)**; darkness and oppression **(2 Cor. 4:4; 2 Pet. 1:4-9)**;

deadness and weakness **(Heb. 6:1; 9:14)** delay and compromise **(Acts 24:25; 26:28)**; and divisions and strife **(1 Pet. 5:8; 1 Cor. 3:1-3)**. This list is not even a drop in the bucked. The list of Satan methods of fighting spiritual warfare is much, much to numerous to list or even imagine. The Bible says in **Matt. 7:13**, *"...For wide is the gate, and broad is the way, that leadeth to destruction, and many there be which go in thereat."*

Satan Was Defeated By Jesus Christ

The defeat of Satan and his hosts was accomplished by Christ at the first advent as far as redemption of the race and the Earth is concerned, and this defeat made possible the final suppression of all rebellion and the final defeat of Satan's kingdom at the second coming of Christ. Paul says that Christ on the cross *"spoiled principalities and powers, he made a shew of them openly, triumphing over them in it"* **(Col. 2:14-17)**. Christ on the cross said, *"It is finished"* **(John 19:30),** that is, the work that God had given Christ to finish at His first advent **(John 17:4)**. This work was the actual work of atonement and of completing the redemption for all who believe, but the final work of Christ is yet to come at the second advent. At that time God will send Him from Heaven with an army from Heaven sufficiently large enough and powerful enough to seize the kingdoms of this world in one day and set up a righteous government on the Earth for the purpose of ridding the Earth of all rebels **(Zech. 14:1-21; Rev. 11:15; 19:11-20:10; 1 Cor. 15:24-28; Jude 14; 2 Thess. 1:7-10)**.

All that remains to be done is the suppression of all rebellion on the Earth. The purpose of the thousand-years reign of Christ is to suppress all rebellion **(1 Cor. 15:24-28)**; and the final defeat of Satan and his hosts at the end of the Millennium must be accomplished before the Earth is rid of all rebels. They must be confined to the lake of fire forever before rebellion is finally and eternally overcome.

The Difference Between Jesus and Satan

Angels were the first to help God administer the affairs of the universe **(Col. 1:15-18)**. Lucifer, himself, ruled this planet and through pride fell and invaded Heaven to dethrone God (Luke 10:18), but was defeated and his kingdom destroyed and the Earth placed under water and darkness. Lucifer's highest ambition was to *"be like the Most High"* in the infinite and sovereign sense.

This spirit of pride and self-exaltation was the very opposite of what the second person of the Godhead demonstrated when He emptied Himself and thought it not something to be grasped after to retain equality with God. Since Lucifer fell he has become the leader of all whose program is self-exaltation and rule-or-ruin. Some day he will be forced to capitulate and bow the knees to Him who demonstrated the opposite principle, who emptied and humbled Himself from deity to humanity and from humanity to infamy and who has been exalted at the right hand of the Father waiting until His enemies be made His footstool **(Phil. 2:9-11; Ps. 110:1; 1 Cor. 15:22-28; Heb. 2:7-10; 10:12-13; 1 Pet. 3:22)**. In this we have a clear demonstration of the power of the greater and more God like principles of right over wrong, unselfishness over selfishness, humility over pride, faithfulness and obedience over rebellion, and self-emptying over self-exaltation.

Christ came as a man, a lowly servant of all to set the right example of how men can be like God. He came and lived as God would live among men so that men could learn to live like God. He literally **"emptied Himself"** and took the form of a servant instead of the form of a sovereign God. He humbled Himself from deity to humanity and from humanity to infamy, taking on Him the sins of the world and redeeming fallen man to His original dominion.

Satan Final Defeat

There are many Scriptures revealing the coming defeat of Satan and all rebels and of their eternal confinement in eternal Hell: His defeat and doom are prophetically foretold. The first prediction is the first prophecy in the Bible: *"15I will put enmity between thee and the woman, and between thy seed and her seed; it [the Messiah, the seed of the woman] shall bruise his head, and thou shalt bruise his heel"* **(Gen. 3:15)**.

Isaiah predicted that when the Messiah shall come the second time, Satan will be defeated and he and his hosts put in the abyss: *"And it shall come to pass IN THAT DAY [a phrase referring to the Millennium or the day of the Lord], that the Lord will punish the host of the high ones that are on high, and the kings of the earth upon the earth. And they shall be gathered together, as prisoners are gathered in the pit, and shall be shut up in prison, and after many days [1,000 years according to* **Rev. 20:1-10**] *shall they be visited. THEN [in that day] the moon shall be confounded, and the sun* **ashamed,** **WHEN** *the Lord of hosts shall reign in mount Zion, and in Jerusalem, and before his ancients gloriously"* **(Isa. 24:21-23; 25:6-8).**

In the book of Revelation John predicts that Satan and all of his angels will be cast out of the heavenlies to the Earth in the middle of Daniel's Seventieth Week **(Rev. 12:7-12);** that he will be on Earth the last three and one-half years of this **(Rev. 12:3-14);** that he will cause the greatest trouble that ever has been on Earth **(Rev. 12:13-17; Matt. 24:15-31);** that he will give his power to the antichrist for forty-two months **(Rev. 13:1-7);** that he will mobilize the nations at Armageddon to fight against Christ at His second advent **(Rev. 16:13-16);** that he will fight against Christ at Armageddon and will be taken bodily and be bound in a chain and cast into the abyss for 1,000 years **(Rev. 19:11-20:3);** and that at the end of the 1,000 years he will be loosed out of the abyss and will lead one more rebellion in the Kingdom of God, and then he will be cast bodily into the lake of fire forever **(Rev. 20:7-10; Matt. 25:31).**

**May God Bless You And Keep You
In My Prayer In Jesus Name.**

CPSIA information can be obtained
at www.ICGtesting.com
Printed in the USA
BVHW090053020822
643542BV00011B/979